The Dorset
WOMEN'S INSTITUTE
COOKERY BOOK

DORSET BOOKS

First published in Great Britain in 1990 by Dorset Books

ISBN: 1-871164-09-5

British Library Cataloguing-in-Publication Data
The Dorset Women's Institute cookery book.
1. Food – Recipes
I. Dorset Federation of Women's Institutes
641.5
Typesetting by P&M Typesetting Ltd, Exeter
Printed and bound in Great Britain by BPCC Wheatons Ltd

DORSET BOOKS
An imprint of Wheaton Publishers Ltd.
A Member of the Maxwell Communication Corporation plc

Wheaton Publishers Ltd
Hennock Road, Marsh Barton, Exeter, Devon EX2 8RP
Tel: 0392 74121; Telex 42794 (WHEATN G)

SALES
Direct sales enquiries to Dorset Books at the address above.

Cover photograph: The mill at Sturminster Newton (Courtesy of Peter Speed)

FOREWORD

This new Dorset WI Cookery book is compiled from favourite recipes of the members of the WI in Dorset. I hope you are tempted to try these very interesting recipes. Some have been brought back by members after sojourns abroad, some are very British recipes but with exciting and unusual ingredients.

Our thanks are due to those members who sent recipes in and to the team who collated them. Also we would like to thank Dorset Books for all their help and co-operation in the production of this book.

Happy Cooking!

Margaret Gibson

Margaret Gibson

Chairman
Dorset Federation of Women's Institutes

PREFACE

DORSET FEDERATION OF WOMEN'S INSTITUTES

There are over 180 Institutes in Dorset, and the members are friendly, go-ahead, like-minded women, who get enormous pleasure from their activities and from all that the WI has to offer. They enjoy the monthly meetings and companionship, going on outings together, taking part in such activities as drama, crafts, debates and skittles, to name but a few. There are two big meetings a year, when members get together with others from all over the county, and also two group meetings a year when five or six Institutes get together. There are various events organized by the county sub-committees, when everyone has the chance to participate. There is also the Annual General Meeting, when representatives from all over the country meet.

The WI is the largest women's organization in the country, and the only one with its own adult education establishment. This is Denman College, where there are courses on anything from car maintenance to paper sculpture, microwave cookery to fly-fishing, dress-making to current affairs.

There are WI markets throughout the country which sell cakes, flowers, plants, eggs, jams, crafts and many other items. For a small fee you can become a shareholder and producer.

There is an Institute near you. Why not join us? For further information contact the Dorset Federation of Women's Institutes, County Office, Princes Street, Dorchester, tel. 0305 266366, or the National Federation of Women's Institutes, 39 Eccleston Street, London SW1W 9NT, tel. 01 730 7212.

CONTENTS

TEMPERATURE AND WEIGHT CHARTS, QUANTITY GUIDE AND NOTES ON RECIPES

OVEN CHART	Approximate Temperature Centre Oven		Heat of Oven
Gas Mark	Fahrenheit	Celsius	
¼	225°	110°	Very Cool
½	250°	120°	
1	275°	130°	Cool
2	300°	150°	
3	325°	160°	Warm
4	350°	180°	Moderate
5	375°	190°	Fairly Hot
6	400°	200°	
7	425°	220°	Hot
8	450°	230°	Very Hot
9	475°	250°	

NOTES ON METRICATION

Ounces/fluid ounces	Approx. g. and ml. to nearest whole figure	Recommended conversion to nearest unit of 25
1	28	25
2	57	50
3	85	75
4	113	125
5 (¼ pint)	142	150
6	170	175
7	198	200
8	227	225
9	255	250
10 (½ pint)	283	275
16 (1 lb.)	454	450
20 (1 pint)	567	575

As general guide, 1 kg. (1000 g.) equals 2.2 lb. or about 2 lb 3 oz.
1 litre (1000 ml.) equals 1.76 pints or just over 1¾ pints.

QUANTITY GUIDE

BREAD

Sandwich loaf, large thin-sliced	– gives approx. 24 slices
Brown bread, large sliced	– gives approx. 18 slices
French stick, long	– cuts into approx. 20 × 1 in. slices

BUTTER

¼ lb., softened	– spreads 1 large sliced loaf
½ lb., softened	– spreads 24 bread rolls
½ lb., softened	– spreads 50 small bridge rolls
½ oz. portion	– per individual serving for rolls and biscuits

CAKES AND GATEAUX

1 × 8 in. round sponge cake	– cuts into 6–8 portions
1 × 12 in. round sponge cake	– cuts into 12–16 portions
1 × 9 in. square fruit cake	– cuts into 16–20 slices
1 × 12 in. square fruit cake	– cuts into 40–50 slices

CHEESE

4 oz. per person	– cheese and wine party
2 oz. per person	– ploughman's
1 oz. per person	– after dinner
2 lb. grated	– 36 full sandwich rounds

CHEESE BISCUITS   – allow 3 per person after dinner

CREAM   – 1 fl. oz per portion

DRINKS

Coffee, instant	– 2 oz. per 8 pints water
	– makes 30 cups
Coffee, fresh	– 2 oz. per 2 pints water
	– makes 10 small cups
Tea, bags	– 10 bags per 8 pints water
	– makes approx. 32 cups
Tea, leaves	– 1½ oz. per 8 pints water
	– makes approx. 32 cups
Milk	– 2 pints per 8 pints of tea

EGGS

24 hard-boiled (with mayonnaise)	– 36 full sandwich rounds

7

FRUIT
Soft fruits and grapes   – 2–3 oz. per portion

MEATS
Sliced, cold   – 3 oz. per portion
Sliced, hot   – 4 oz. per portion
2 lb. sliced cold meat   – 36 full sandwich rounds
3 ½ lb. uncooked chicken   – gives 6 portions

PASTA
2 oz. uncooked   – per portion

PASTRY (flour weights)
6 oz. shortcrust   – lines 1 × 8in. flan ring
8 oz. shortcrust   – lines 1 × 12 in. flan ring
4 oz. choux   – makes 40 profiteroles
                            (3 per portion)

PASTRY (prepared weight), frozen
13 oz. pack puff pastry   – makes 20 × 2 in. vol au vent cases
7 ½ oz. pack shortcrust   – lines 1 × 7 in.–8 in. flan ring

PUDDINGS
Fruit salad, canned 5 varieties   – 5 × 1 lb. 13 oz. cans per 25
                            portions
Fruit salad, fresh 5 varieties   – 4 oz. per portion
Meringues, 10 egg whites,   – 50–75 according to size
  1 pt. cream   (2 shells per portion)

RICE
Uncooked, main course   – 2 oz. per portion
Cooked, salad use   – 2 oz. per portion

SALAD DRESSINGS
Mayonnaise   – ½ pint per 10–12 portions
Oil and vinegar   – ½ pint per 12–14 portions,
                            – ½ pint dresses mixed salad for 20
                            portions

SALADS (quantities based on 3 different salads being offered)
Coleslaw   – 2 oz. per portion
Potato   – 3 oz. per portion
Lettuce – 1 medium   – 6–7 portions

Mixed green salad – 1 lettuce, 1 pepper, 4 in. cucumber, 1 bunch watercress	– 6–8 portions
Mixed vegetable salad	– 2 oz. total mixture per portion
Tomatoes, sliced	– 1 lb. per 6–8 portions
Watercress	– 1 bunch per 6–8 portions

SCONES

½ lb. flour weight	– 2½ in. cutter cuts 9–10 rounds – 1¾ in.–2 in. cutter cuts 16-18 rounds
Jam – 1 lb.	– approx. 4–5 dozen scones
Cream – 5 fl. oz.	– approx. 25 scones

SOUP

1 pint	– 3 portions

VEGETABLES

Most varieties, prepared weight	– 2 oz. per portion, if serving 2 varieties – 3 oz. per portion, if serving 1 variety
Potatoes, prepared weight	– 3 oz. per portion

SOME BASIC RECIPES REFERRED TO IN THE BOOK

Basic White Sauce (Method)

Melt butter, stir in flour and cook for 1 minute.
Remove from heat and add milk/liquid a little at a time, stirring well to blend.
Return to heat and stir until thickened.

Shortcrust Pastry (To make 8 oz.)

4 oz. fat (butter or margarine/lard mix)
8 oz. plain flour
Water

Rub the fat into the flour until it resembles breadcrumbs.
Gradually add cold water, a little at a time until it forms a stiff dough.
Roll out on a floured surface.

Meringues (Method to make approx. 20)

Whisk 3 egg whites until stiff. Add 6 oz. caster sugar, a tablespoon at a time, whisking well after each addition. Finally add 1 teaspoon of lemon juice.
Pipe or spoon about 20 on to lined baking sheets. Bake for 2–3 hours at 225°F/110°C/Gas Mark ¼. Change the positions of the trays in the oven half way through the cooking time.

QUANTITIES GUIDE – DRINKS

QUANTITY IN NUMBER OF BOTTLES

	25	50	100	People
Sherry 12–15 glasses per 75 cl. bottle 1 glass per head	3	5	8–9	
Sparkling wine/Champagne 6 glasses per 75 cl. bottle 2 glasses per head	8–9	16–17	30–33	Bottles
Still wine approx. ½ × 75 cl. bottle per head	13	20–25	40–50	

Spirits one bottle will serve 32 singles
Soft drinks 1 pint per head

TABLE OF ROUX-BASED SAUCE CONSISTENCIES

Type of Sauce	Fat	Flour	Milk or other liquid	Use
Thin Sauce	½ oz.	½ oz.	½ pint	Base for soups
Pouring sauce	¾ oz.	¾ oz.	½ pint	For fish, meat vegetables and sweet dishes
Coating sauce	1 oz.	1 oz.	½ pint	Coating foods
Panada (very thick sauce)	2 oz.	2 oz.	½ pint	To bind foods, base for soufflés

EGGS

Sizes one-two (3–2 ½ oz.) are large.
Sizes three-four (2 ½–2 oz.) are standard.
Sizes five-six (2–1 ¾ oz.) are small.

SPOON MEASURES

Flour	3 level tablespoons = 1 oz.
All types of sugar (except icing sugar)	2 level tablespoons = 1 oz.
Icing sugar	3 level tablespoons = 1 oz.
Cornflour	3 level tablespoons = 1 oz.
Arrowroot	2 level tablespoons = 1 oz.
Golden syrup/treacle	1 level tablespoon = just under 1 oz.
Milk, water, etc.	2 tablespoons = 1 oz.
	5 tablespoons = ⅛ pint (2½ fl. oz.)
Margarine or butter	2 tablespoons = 1¼ oz.

NOTES ON THE RECIPES

* Indicates that a dish may be frozen.

SOUPS

ARTICHOKE SOUP

Serves 2–3

1 lb approx. Jerusalem artichokes
2 tablespoons butter
2 tablespoons plain flour
½ pint milk
Pinch nutmeg
Salt and pepper

Prepare and slice artichokes and cook for 5–10 minutes in boiling water.
To make sauce, melt butter, stir in flour, cook for 1 minute, gradually
    add milk and stir until boiling.
Drain and then liquidize or mash the artichokes (depending on how
    smooth you want the soup to be). Add to the sauce.
Add nutmeg and season to taste.

To make a meal, top with grated cheese and serve with toast.

CARROT SOUP

Serves 3

5 oz. carrot, chopped
5 oz. onion, chopped
1½ oz. potato, chopped
Pinch mixed herbs
14 fl. oz. vegetable stock
2 teaspoons lemon juice
Salt and pepper

Simmer vegetables, herbs and stock for 30 minutes.
Blend or process until smooth.
Return to saucepan, bring to boil and add lemon juice and seasoning.

Serve with grated cheese and warm French bread.

CARROT AND LEEK SOUP

Serves 4

2 carrots
2 large leeks
1 oz. butter
1 teaspoon horseradish sauce
10 oz. medium oatmeal
Salt and pepper to taste
Mace or bay leaf
1 pint vegetable stock
¼ pint milk

Slice carrots and leeks thinly, and sauté in butter for 7 minutes.
Add all other ingredients, bring to the boil and simmer for 25 minutes.

CELERY SOUP WITH TOASTED ALMONDS

Serves 4

1 large head of celery
2 oz. butter
1 pint chicken stock
Salt and pepper
Freshly grated nutmeg
15 fl. oz. milk
5 oz. yogurt (or cream)
2 tablespoons finely chopped parsley (optional)
1 oz. flaked almonds, toasted

Wash, dry and chop celery.
Heat the butter in a heavy-bottomed saucepan and add celery.
Cover and cook over a low heat for about 10 minutes, shaking the pan
   from time to time.
Add the chicken stock, salt, pepper and nutmeg. Cover and simmer for
   about 20 minutes.
Add milk and yogurt, and simmer for 5 minutes.
Blend until smooth, and sieve back into the pan to remove any fibres.
Adjust the seasoning, reheat, stir in parsley and sprinkle almonds on
   top just before serving.

CHICKEN SOUP

Serves 4

1¾ pints good chicken stock
1 large carrot, peeled and coarsely grated
1 medium-sized turnip (or swede), peeled and coarsely grated
2 leeks, washed, trimmed and finely shredded
4 oz. firm cabbage, finely shredded
2 oz. cooked chicken, shredded
2 tablespoons chopped fresh parsley
Salt and ground black pepper

Bring stock to the boil, add vegetables and simmer for 15 minutes.
Add chicken and parsley and simmer for 5 minutes, until the vegetables
    are cooked.
Season to taste.

Serve with warm crusty bread and grated cheese.

GREEK BEAN SOUP

Serves 3

8 oz. dried beans (haricot or butter)
3 carrots, sliced
3 sticks celery, sliced
2 large onions, sliced
¼ pint olive oil (or vegetable oil)
14 oz. can tomatoes
1–2 teaspoons tomato paste
Generous handful of chopped parsley

Black pepper (plenty)
1 tablespoon fresh oregano
    (½ teaspoon dried)
1 tablespoon fresh thyme
    (½ teaspoon dried)
Salt

Soak the beans overnight. Rinse and cover with water. Bring to the boil
    for about 5 minutes, then strain and reheat in fresh water.
Add all the ingredients except half the chopped parsley and any salt
    (always cook pulses in unsalted water until almost tender, as salt
    toughens their texture and adds to the cooking time). Simmer for
    about 1½ hours, until the beans are soft and the soup is thick and
    almost creamy in consistency. Add salt to taste and sprinkle on the
    rest of the chopped parsley.

Eaten with chunks of wholemeal or granary bread, this makes a
    perfectly satisfying meal in itself.

13

MUSHROOM SOUP

Serves 4

8 oz. mushrooms
2 oz. butter
2 tablespoons plain flour
15 fl. oz. chicken stock
5 fl. oz. milk
2 tablespoons chopped parsley
Juice of half a lemon
5 fl. oz. thick cream
Salt and ground black pepper

Prepare and chop mushrooms and blend to a purée.
Melt butter in a saucepan, add flour and cook gently for 3–4 minutes.
    Stir in stock a little at a time. Bring to the boil, stirring all the time to
    blend smoothly.
Add the milk, mushrooms, parsley and lemon juice and cook for 5
    minutes.
Stir in cream and season to taste.

PARSLEY SOUP

Serves 3

2 oz. parsley
1 bunch watercress
1½ oz. butter (or margarine)
1 medium potato, sliced
1½ pints stock
5 fl. oz. plain yogurt
1 teaspoon plain flour

Sauté parsley and watercress in butter for 10 minutes. Add potato and
    cook for ½ minute. Add stock and simmer for 20 minutes. Cool,
    liquidize and return to pan.
Mix yogurt and flour and add to pan. Reheat before serving.

PEA SOUP

Serves 6–8

1½ lb. dried peas
2 lb. belly pork
1 lb. carrots, chopped
1 lb. potatoes, diced
Large onion, chopped
Head of celery, chopped
2–3 leeks, finely sliced
1–1½ teaspoons dried thyme

Soak peas overnight.
Boil pork until almost cooked (about 45 minutes) in 2½ pints of water.
  Remove pork from pan, reserving liquid, and chop into small pieces.
Add all ingredients to the pork liquor, and cook for 15–20 minutes, until
  tender.
Season to taste.

SUPPER SOUP

Serves 4

1–1½ lb. scrag end of lamb (depending on how meaty it is)
2 carrots, diced
2 sticks celery, cut in ½ in. pieces
2 medium potatoes, diced
1 medium onion, sliced
2 oz. pearl barley
1¾ pints stock
Salt and pepper

Cook all ingredients at high pressure in pressure-cooker for 20 minutes.
  Reduce pressure under running tap.
Take out lamb. Cut meat into small chunks, removing the bones, and
  return to the pan.
Reheat before serving.

Serve with chunks of French bread. Follow with a green salad.

15

WATERCRESS SOUP

Serves 4–6

1¾ oz. butter
1 medium onion, finely chopped
2 bunches watercress
1½ pints chicken stock
Salt and pepper
¾ oz. plain flour
4 tablespoons thick cream

Melt 1 oz. butter in large heavy-bottomed saucepan, add onion and
cook over moderate heat until soft.
Wash and dry the watercress, and discard the lower third of the stalks.
Add to the onion. Cover the pan and sweat the watercress for 5
minutes, shaking the pan occasionally.
Add stock and simmer for 10 minutes. Season to taste.
Liquidize, return to pan and bring to boil.
Mash the remaining butter and the flour together to make a *beurre manié*,
and add to the soup a little at a time, whisking vigorously so that it
does not form lumps.
Simmer for 2–3 minutes until it has thickened.
Stir in the cream before serving.

Garnish with lime or lemon slices.

STARTERS

AVOCADOS WITH CRAB

Serves 4

2 ripe avocados, cut in half and stones removed
3 oz. tin crab meat, drained
½ red pepper, finely chopped
1 tablespoon lemon juice (use more if wanted)
3 tablespoons salad oil
½ teaspoon French mustard
½ clove garlic, crushed
2 tablespoons tomato chutney
1 tablespoon finely chopped parsley
Salt and pepper to taste

Flake the crab meat with a fork in a bowl. Mix in red pepper.
Mix remaining ingredients together and stir into the crab meat mixture.
    Add more lemon juice if wanted.
Spoon into avocado halves.

AVOCADOS STUFFED WITH DANISH BLUE CHEESE

Serves 4

2 avocados
2 teaspoons lemon juice

2 oz. Danish Blue cheese
2 tablespoons curd cheese

Halve the avocados. Remove stone and some of the flesh leaving ½ in.
    thick shells.
Mash avocado flesh and lemon juice and blend in cheeses and salt and
    pepper to taste.
Pile mixture into shells and chill.

Garnish with parsley.

17

CHEESE POTS

Serves 2

2 oz. Cheddar cheese finely grated
1½ oz. Blue Stilton cheese
1 oz. butter
2 tablespoons milk

1 small clove garlic, crushed
1 teaspoon chopped chives
Salt and pepper

Beat Stilton and butter in a bowl until blended. Add rest of ingredients.
  Mix well.
Put into pots and chill.

Garnish with parsley and serve with toast.

CRISPY EGG AND TUNA

Serves 2–3

3½ oz. tin tuna
2 tablespoons sweetcorn
2 hard-boiled eggs, chopped
½ oz. butter
2 tablespoons plain flour

5 fl. oz. milk
2 oz. grated cheese
2 teaspoons chives, chopped
1 packet potato crisps, crushed

Pre-heat oven to 350°F/180°C/Gas Mark 4.
Layer tuna, sweetcorn and egg in ovenproof dish.
Make sauce with butter, flour and milk (for method see page 9), add
  grated cheese and chives and season to taste. Pour over tuna layers.
Sprinkle with crisps and bake for 30 minutes.

Serve hot garnished with chopped chives.

FRESH MACKEREL STARTER

Serves 4

1 onion, finely chopped
4 fresh mackerel fillets, cut into 1 in. slices
Dry red wine (or cider)
Breadcrumbs, fresh
½ oz. butter (or oil)
Salt and pepper

Pre-heat oven to 350°F/180°C/Gas Mark 4.
Heat butter in ovenproof dish, add onion and cook for 5 minutes.
Add fish and wine, sprinkle breadcrumbs over and add seasoning.
Dot with butter. Cook for 10 minutes or until the fish is done.

HUNGARIAN POTTED CHEESE

Serves 4

5 oz. unsalted butter
8 oz. cream cheese
1 teaspoon German (or French) mustard
4 teaspoons paprika
2 tablespoons beer

1 teaspoon grated onion
½ teaspoon caraway seeds
1 teaspoon chopped parsley
1 teaspoon chopped chives
Salt and pepper

Cream butter and then work in other ingredients. Put into pots and
  chill.
Serve with toast.

HUNTER'S PÂTÉ

Serves 16

1 lb. rabbit or hare flesh
1 lb. trimmed belly pork
½ lb. pig's liver
1 lb. pork sausagemeat
½ lb. garlic sausage
4 oz. onion, skinned and chopped
3 tablespoons sherry
1 lb. fat streaky bacon rashers, with rind removed

2 tablespoons chopped parsley
2 level tablespoons dried sage
Salt and black pepper

Pre-heat oven to 325°F/160°C/Gas Mark 3.
Cut rabbit or hare into small pieces.
Put the pork, liver, sausagemeat, garlic sausage and onion through a
  mincer. Mix in the rabbit or hare pieces and add sherry, parsley and
  sage. Season well.
Line a large loaf tin with bacon rashers. Turn the pâté mixture into the
  prepared tin and fold the bacon edges over the top.
Cover with foil and place in a roasting tin containing enough water to
  come half-way up.
Cook in oven for 3 hours. Allow to cool in tin.

KIPPER PÂTÉ

Serves 4

7 oz. packet cook-in-bag kipper fillets
4 oz. cream cheese
1 teaspoon horseradish sauce
2 oz. butter
2 oz. yogurt
Cayenne and black pepper to taste
Melted butter to cover when potted.

½ clove garlic, crushed
Juice of half a lemon

Cook kippers as instructed, skin and remove any bones.
Process all ingredients.
Pot into individual ramekins.
Cover with melted butter, chill.

Serve with toast.

LEICESTER FISH PÂTÉ*

Serves 4

7 oz. tin tuna fish
7 oz. Red Leicester cheese, grated
1 teaspoon lemon juice

5 oz. natural yogurt
2 tablespoons chopped parsley
Ground black pepper

Drain tuna, mash well and place in a bowl with the cheese and lemon
    juice. Mix well.
Beat in the yogurt, parsley and pepper.
Press the mixture into one large or four individual dishes.

Garnish with sprigs of parsley and serve with crispbreads, rolls or
    French bread.

MUSHROOM AND EGG MOUSSE

Serves 2–3 for lunch, 4 as a starter

4 eggs
½ lb. button mushrooms
1 heaped tablespoon butter
Salt and pepper

2 teaspoons powdered gelatine
3–4 tablespoons mayonnaise
½ pint double cream
Pinch curry powder

Hard-boil the eggs.

Slice mushrooms thinly, and simmer in butter with seasoning until cooked.

Put gelatine and 6 teaspoons water in a cup and stir until dissolved completely – it should be clear and rather syrupy in consistency.

Mince the eggs and mushrooms together (or use blender but do not let mixture become too smooth). Add mayonnaise and stir in the dissolved gelatine.

Whisk cream until stiff, and curry powder and fold into egg and mushroom mixture. Taste and adjust seasoning. Pile into dish or mould and leave to set.

Garnish with a little paprika.

PRAWN PÂTÉ

Serves 4

4 oz. butter
1 clove garlic, crushed
1 teaspoon ground coriander
4 oz. peeled prawns
3 tablespoons cream (whipping or double)
Salt and pepper

Melt butter over low heat and cook garlic and coriander for 2–3 minutes. Add prawns and toss in the butter. Process or blend till smooth. Add cream and mix briefly. Season to taste, and chill.

Serve with toast.

SMOKED MACKEREL PÂTÉ

Serves 4

8 oz. smoked mackerel
5 oz. natural yogurt
1 tablespoon horseradish sauce
Dash of lemon juice

Skin and flake mackerel. Blend or process with other ingredients until smooth. Pot and chill.

FISH

BAKED TUNA

Serves 8

14 oz. tin tuna, drained
2 tablespoons butter (or margarine)
2 tablespoons plain flour
16 fl. oz. milk
Salt, pepper, paprika
Topping:
    8 tablespoons grated-cheese-and-breadcrumb mixture

2 bay leaves
8 oz. fresh breadcrumbs
4 hard-boiled eggs, chopped
6 tablespoons lemon juice
2 teaspoons Worcester sauce

Pre-heat oven to 350°F/180°C/Gas Mark 4.
Flake tuna.
Make a white sauce with the butter, flour, milk and seasonings,
    removing the bay leaves at the end.
Add tuna, breadcrumbs, egg and lemon juice. Mix well.
Fill medium casserole or eight baking shells, and sprinkle with topping.
Bake for about 30 minutes, until golden brown.

Salmon or crab can be used instead of tuna.
Cooked mixture may also be served cold on crackers or toast as a
    cocktail savoury.

CRAB AU GRATIN

Serves 4

1 oz. butter
1 oz. cornflour
½ pint milk
1 bay leaf
2 oz. cheese, grated

Few drops soy sauce
Salt and pepper
Pinch of cayenne pepper
1 lb. fresh crab meat

Make white sauce with the butter, cornflour, milk and bay leaf (for
    method see page 9).

Add cheese, soy sauce, seasoning and crab meat and mix well. Heat through thoroughly.

Serve in four well-scrubbed scallop shells, garnished with parsley and prawns.

FISH DISH

Serves 4

2 lb. fresh haddock or cod
2 tins condensed mushroom soup
2 oz. butter (or margarine)
1 medium onion, finely chopped
2 packets potato crisps, crushed
2 oz. cheese, grated
1 tomato, sliced

Pre-heat oven to 350°F/180°C/Gas Mark 4.
Cut fish into pieces, place in large baking dish and cover with the mushroom soup.
Melt butter and stir in onion, crisps and cheese. Sprinkle on top of fish mixture.
Bake for 1 hour, putting tomato slices on top for last 15 minutes.

FISH AND PRAWN MOUSSE

Serves 6–8

1 lb. smoked fish (haddock, cod or mackerel)
¼ pint mayonnaise
1 tablespoon tomato purée
1 large lemon
½ oz. gelatine
Salt and pepper
4 oz. peeled prawns (or shrimps)
¼ pint whipped cream
1 egg white, stiffly whisked

Skin and bone the fish, and blend with the mayonnaise and tomato purée until creamy.
Cut four thin slices from the middle of the lemon for garnish, and then add 2 tablespoons lemon juice and 2 teaspoons grated rind to the fish mixture.

Dissolve the gelatine in ¼ pint hot water and place over a pan of hot water until it clears. Blend into the fish mixture with the seasoning and most of the prawns.

Fold in the whipped cream and egg white.

Arrange the remaining prawns at the bottom of a 1 ½–2 pint mould, and spoon in the mixture. Chill until set.

Turn out and garnish with cucumber and mustard and cress.

MACARONI AND HADDOCK AU GRATIN

Serves 6

4 oz. short cut macaroni
1 lb. smoked haddock
¾ pint milk
2 oz. butter (or margarine)
1½ oz. plain flour
2 hard-boiled eggs, sliced
6 oz. Cheddar cheese, grated
2–3 tablespoons breadcrumbs

Cook macaroni until tender, about 7 minutes.

Poach the haddock in the milk about 8–10 minutes. Once cooked, remove from liquid and flake. Reserve the liquid.

Make a sauce with 1 ½ oz. of the butter, the flour and the fish liquid (made up to ¾ pint again). For method see page 9.

Add the macaroni, fish, eggs and 4 oz. of the cheese. Heat 2–3 minutes.

Season well and put in a heatproof dish. Top it with a mixture of the remaining butter and cheese and the breadcrumbs, and brown under the grill.

PLAICE WITH ROMAN SAUCE

Serves 4

Plaice for 4 people
Black pepper
1 lemon, juice (and grated rind for the sauce)

Sauce:
  3 oz. butter
  4 spring onions, chopped
  5 oz. tin anchovies, chopped
  2 tablespoons capers

Pre-heat oven to 350°F/180°C/Gas Mark 4.

Lightly butter pieces of foil, one for each piece of fish.

Position fish on foil, season with pepper and sprinkle with the juice of half the lemon.

Seal the foil. Bake for 25–30 minutes, depending on the thickness of the fish.

Just before the fish is cooked, make the sauce. Melt the butter in small saucepan and soften the onions for 1–2 minutes without browning them. Add the grated lemon rind and rest of juice, the anchovies and the capers.

When fish is ready, split open the parcels and pour the sauce over.

Serve in the foil, garnished with parsley.

SEAFOOD RISOTTO

Serves 4

2 tablespoons cooking oil
Large onion, chopped
Clove garlic, finely chopped
1 cup long-grain rice
Boiling water
3 dried red chillies, finely chopped (optional)
1 chicken stock cube
2 cups frozen mixed vegetables
1 cup frozen peeled prawns
1 cup frozen mussels and/or small scallops
2 small frozen plaice fillets, chopped

Fry onion. Add garlic and rice and stir-fry until rice becomes opaque.

Add water to cover, chillies and stock cube. Bring to boil then simmer, adding more water as necessary.

When nearly cooked, add the rest of the ingredients and cook for a further 10 minutes or so, until vegetables and fish are ready.

Garnish with chopped coriander leaves or parsley.

STUFFED HADDOCK PARCELS

Haddock steaks (one per person)
Stuffing for each steak:
  1 tablespoon parsley and thyme stuffing
  2 tablespoons boiling water
  ½ oz. grated cheese
  Salt and pepper
Butter (for buttering foil)
Sauce:
  2 tablespoons mayonnaise   ½ teaspoon dried thyme
  2 tablespoons natural yogurt   Salt and pepper
  2 teaspoons chopped parsley

Pre-heat oven to 375°F/190°C/Gas Mark 5.
Place stuffing mix in bowl and add boiling water. Stir in cheese and salt
    and pepper.
Place each steak on a piece of buttered foil. Top with stuffing, dot with
    butter and seal foil.
Bake for 20–25 minutes.
Fold back foil and continue to cook for 5–10 minutes, until topping is
    golden.
Blend all sauce ingredients together and serve separately.

TUNA MOUSSE (1)

Serves 6

6 oz. tin tuna, drained
2 eggs, beaten
¼ pint milk
4 oz. cheddar cheese, grated
4 tablespoons mayonnaise
1 stick celery, finely chopped
Salt and pepper

Pre-heat oven to 300°F/150°C/Gas Mark 2.
Mash tuna in a basin, then add all other ingredients and mix
    thoroughly.
Place in six buttered ovenproof dishes and smooth tops. Bake for
    approx. 40 minutes.

Serve hot or cold, garnished with lemon wedges and parsley.

TUNA MOUSSE (2)

Serves 6–8

Sauce:

1 oz. margarine
1 oz. plain flour
½ pint milk
15 oz. tin tuna, drained and flaked
1 egg, separated
¼ pint mayonnaise

1 dessertspoon lemon juice
Salt and pepper
½ oz. gelatine
3 tablespoons water

Oil inside of dish or mould.
Make sauce (for method see page 9), and stir in fish. Leave to cool.
Stir in egg yolk, mayonnaise, lemon juice and salt and pepper.
Dissolve gelatine in the water, and stir into the mixture.
Whisk egg white stiffly and fold in.
Turn into oiled dish and leave to set.

Turn out of dish and garnish with lemon and cucumber.

TUNA NOODLE CASSEROLE

Serves 4–6

8 oz. noodles
1 or 2 small tins tuna, drained
½ cup mayonnaise
1 cup sliced celery
⅓ cup chopped onion
3 oz. peas or 1 small chopped green pepper or 2 oz. mushrooms
1 teaspoon salt
¼ teaspoon pepper
1 tin condensed celery soup
½ cup milk
1 cup grated cheese

Pre-heat oven to 425°F/220°C/Gas Mark 7.
Cook noodles in boiling salted water. Drain.
Combine noodles, tuna, mayonnaise, vegetables and seasoning.
Blend soup and milk and heat through. Add cheese and heat until
    cheese melts. Add to noodle mix.
Bake for 20 minutes.

CHICKEN

BARBECUE CHICKEN WINGS

Serves 6

12 chicken wings
2 tablespoons oil
½ cup diced onion
1 clove garlic, finely chopped
1 cup diced celery
1 cup diced red and green pepper
¾ cup water

1 cup tomato ketchup
2 tablespoons lemon juice
2 tablespoons Worcester sauce
2 tablespoons brown sugar
1 tablespoon dry mustard
1 teaspoon salt
¼ teaspoon pepper

Pre-heat oven to 325°F/160°C/Gas Mark 3.
Cut off tops of wings.
Heat oil in deep saucepan and brown wings slowly, a few at a time.
    Remove wings.
Fry onion and garlic until transparent.
Return wings to pan.
Mix together the remaining ingredients and pour them over the wings.
    Bring to the boil and simmer for 10 minutes.
Pour chicken mixture into casserole and bake for 1 hour, until tender.
Serve with rice or mashed potatoes

CHICKEN ADOBO

Serves 6

6–12 chicken pieces (depending on size)
1 tablespoon finely chopped garlic
5 tablespoons soy sauce
5 fl. oz. distilled malt vinegar

15 fl. oz. water
1 bay leaf
1 teaspoon salt
½ teaspoon whole peppercorns

Put everything into a large saucepan – the chicken should be almost
    covered by the water. Bring to the boil with the lid on, then reduce
    heat and simmer gently for 30 minutes.
Uncover and simmer for a further 15 minutes, until the chicken is tender
    but not falling off the bones.

Serve with boiled rice.

CHICKEN DIVAN

Serves 6

2 bunches fresh or 2 packets frozen broccoli
3 lb. chicken, cooked and sliced
1 tin condensed chicken soup
1 tin condensed mushroom soup
1 cup low-fat mayonnaise
1 teaspoon lemon juice
1 teaspoon curry powder

Topping:
1 cup grated strong cheese
1 cup breadcrumbs

Pre-heat oven to 350°F/180°C/Gas Mark 4.
Cook broccoli until tender, then drain. Arrange in a large dish and place sliced chicken on top.
Combine all other ingredients and pour over chicken.
Sprinkle with cheese and breadcrumbs and bake until thoroughly heated through.

CHICKEN WITH LEMON AND GRAPES

Serves 4

3–3½ lb. roasting chicken
1 lemon
½ lb. small white seedless grapes
Salt and pepper

1 oz. butter
½ oz. plain flour
6 fl. oz. single cream
1 chicken stock cube

Pre-heat oven to 375°F/190°C/Gas Mark 5.
Peel rind from lemon. Stuff chicken with lemon rind and de-stalked grapes.
Cut lemon in half and use halves to rub over chicken. Season chicken with salt and pepper, place in roasting tin and dot with butter. Roast for at least 1 hour, basting occasionally. After ½ hour, remove the grapes from the chicken with a spoon taking care not to break them.
When cooked, transfer the chicken to a serving dish and keep warm.
To make the sauce, put grapes and all juices in a pan over fierce heat and reduce liquid. Stir flour in quickly, add cream and allow to bubble and thicken. Correct seasoning with crumbled stock cube.
Pour sauce over chicken.

CHICKEN IN ZINGY SAUCE

Serves 4

3–3½ lb. roasting chicken
Sauce:
1½ oz. butter
1½ oz. plain flour
¾ pint chicken stock
2 dessertspoons French mustard
4 oz. grated cheese (preferably Emmental or Gruyère –
reserve a little for sprinkling over the top)
6 fl. oz. single cream

Pre-heat oven to 400°F/200°C/Gas Mark 6.
Roast chicken, allowing 20 minutes per lb.
Make sauce. (For method see page 9. Add cheese, mustard and cream
when thickened.) Simmer for 15 minutes until smooth and thick.
Meanwhile, remove meat from bird and put it in large pieces in a fairly
shallow dish.
Pour over the sauce, sprinkle with the remaining cheese and return to
the oven for 20 minutes.

Garnish with parsley and serve with green salad.

COLD CURRIED CHICKEN

Serves 4

1 lb. cooked chicken,
cut into bite-sized pieces
1 tablespoon olive oil
1 small onion, chopped
1 level tablespoon curry powder
¼ pint stock

1 teaspoon tomato purée
Juice of half a lemon
2 tablespoons sweet chutney
(or apricot jam)
½ pint mayonnaise
3 tablespoons single cream

Fry the onion gently in the oil, covered, for 5 minutes.
Stir in the curry powder and cook for a further few minutes.
Stir in stock, tomato purée, lemon juice and chutney, keep stirring until
boiling, then simmer for 5 minutes.
Take off heat, strain into a basin and leave to cool.
Stir in mayonnaise and cream and use to coat chicken pieces.

Serve with a rice salad.

HAM-STUFFED CHICKEN WITH CRANBERRY MARNIER SAUCE

Serves 8–10

5 lb. oven-ready chicken and a roasting bag
Stuffing:
   Large onion, finely chopped
   1½ oz. butter
   ½ lb. cooked ham, minced or finely chopped
   ½ level teaspoon ground coriander
   1 level teaspoon dried thyme
   5 oz. fresh white breadcrumbs
   Salt and black pepper
   2 eggs, beaten
24 stuffed olives
Sauce:
   1 lb. whole cranberries, fresh or frozen
   8 fl. oz. water
   5 oz. caster sugar
   ½ level teaspoon cinnamon
   3–4 tablespoons Grand Marnier

Bone chicken: Make a cut along backbone from neck to tail. Cut off
   parson's nose and tips of legs. Using a small sharp knife, work flesh
   away from the carcase until you reach the wing socket. Break socket,
   scrape flesh from first bone and cut off joint. The lower bones may be
   left or removed, as preferred. Continue working flesh from carcase
   until you reach the leg. Remove thigh bone. Continue on to breast,
   and carefully cut over breast bone without tearing skin. Do second
   side in same way.
Lay bird skin-side down and make sure flesh is evenly distributed.
   Season lightly.
Pre-heat oven to 350°F/180°C/Gas Mark 4.
Make stuffing: Fry onion in butter until soft but not coloured. Turn into
   a bowl. Mix well with other ingredients except olives.
Lay half the stuffing over the centre of the chicken in a brick shape,
   arrange sixteen olives in two rows along its length and cover them
   with a little more stuffing. Arrange the last eight olives in a row
   between the other two rows and cover with the remaining stuffing.
Fold over the chicken to enclose the stuffing and secure with skewers or
   thread.
Turn bird right way up. Put legs and wings in position and truss lightly.

31

Brush with melted butter, put in roasting bag and cook for 1 ½–2 hours.
Make sauce: Bring cranberries to boil in the water. Simmer gently until
they have all popped, and then for a further 2–3 minutes. Add sugar
and cinnamon and stir until sugar has dissolved. Simmer for about 5
minutes or until thick. Remove from heat, stir in Grand Marnier and
leave to cool.

The chicken can be eaten hot or chilled. The sauce will keep in jars in the
fridge for up to 3 weeks.

PLUSH CHICKEN PIE

Serves 8–10

10–12 chicken pieces
(mixed drumsticks and thighs)
½ lb. mushrooms
1 teaspoon crushed garlic
Bouquet garni
Small carton yogurt

Small carton soured cream
2 oz. flaked almonds
1 oz. plain flour
1 oz. cornflour
1 lb. puff pastry
1 egg, beaten

Pre-heat oven to 400°F/200°C/Gas Mark 6.
Put the chicken, mushrooms, garlic and bouquet garni in a deep
casserole, pour over the yogurt and soured cream and cook until
tender. Allow to cool.
Remove mushrooms and chicken to a bowl, discarding bones and skin.
Add almonds.
Using the flour and cornflour mixed together, thicken the liquor in the
casserole, and add it to the bowl. Stir.
Roll out the puff pastry and make a collar of it around the edges of the
pie dish(es). Pour in the chicken mixture. Use the beaten egg to seal
the pastry top and collar together and brush the top with the
remaining egg. Cook until golden brown.

POULET SOUS LA CLOCHE

Serves 4

1 chicken
½ pint dry white wine (or dry cider)
4 oz. mushrooms
1 bay leaf
Salt and pepper

1½ oz. butter
1½ oz. plain flour
½ pint milk
Tin asparagus (or sweetcorn)

Pre-heat oven to 350°F/180°C/Gas Mark 4.

Lay chicken upside-down in casserole, so that juices run down into breast. Add wine, mushrooms, bay leaf and salt. Cover and cook for about 1 ½ hours.

Make sauce with butter, flour, liquor from casserole (discarding bay leaf) and milk (for method see page 9). Add asparagus and season well.

Carve chicken on to hot serving dish, pour over the sauce and garnish with the mushrooms.

ROAST CHICKEN WITH ORANGE AND WINE

Serves 4

1 roasting chicken
2 oranges
2 tablespoons clear honey
¼ pint white wine

Pre-heat oven to 450°F/230°C/Gas Mark 8.

Prick one orange all over with a skewer and place whole inside the chicken.

Baste the chicken all over with the juice of the other orange, and then with the honey.

Cooking time is 20 minutes per lb. plus 20 minutes. After the first 20 minutes reduce the heat to 375°F/190°C/Gas Mark 5. Twenty minutes before the end of the cooking time pour the wine over the chicken.

SPECIAL CHICKEN SUPREME

Serves 2

2 chicken breasts, skinned and boned
Stuffing:
　½ oz. butter
　2 rashers streaky bacon, snipped into small pieces
　1 shallot, finely chopped
　4 oz. mushrooms, finely chopped
　2 tablespoons fine breadcrumbs
　1 egg white, beaten
　2 tablespoons cream (or yogurt)
A little lemon juice

33

Sauce:

1 oz. butter
¾ oz. plain flour (or cornflour)
½ pint chicken stock
¼ pint single cream
1 egg yolk
A little lemon juice

Make the stuffing: Cook the bacon in the butter for a few minutes, then add shallot and mushrooms and cook until soft. Stir in the breadcrumbs, allow to cool, add egg white and cream and season to taste.

Pre-heat oven to 350°F/180°C/Gas Mark 4.

Slit the chicken breasts and fill with the stuffing. Place each on a well-buttered piece of foil, sprinkle with a little lemon juice and wrap into loose but well-sealed parcels.

Cook for 40–45 minutes.

Make the sauce: Make roux with the butter and flour (for method see page 9). Add the cream slowly, stirring well, then the egg yolk. Add lemon juice, beating until a smooth coating sauce is made. Adjust the seasoning. Add a small knob of butter for gloss and beat again.

Remove chicken from their parcels and coat with the sauce before serving.

Serve in a border of creamed potatoes or rice.

SPICED BUTTERED CHICKEN

Serves 4

1 heaped teaspoon coriander seeds
  (or ½ teaspoon ground coriander)
2 teaspoons green peppercorns
1 large clove garlic, chopped
1 in. piece root ginger, chopped
½ teaspoon salt
2 oz. butter, at room temperature
4 bay leaves
8 chicken thighs

Crush coriander seeds and peppercorns with pestle and mortar. Add garlic and ginger and crush to paste. Work into butter with the salt.

Lift skin from joints and insert the butter mixture, leaving a little to rub on the underside after returning the skin neatly round each joint.

Arrange in an ovenproof dish with half a bay leaf under each, and brush with a little oil. Leave for several hours for the flavours to develop.

Pre-heat oven to 375°F/190°C/Gas Mark 5.

Cook for 45 minutes, basting several times.

Serve with rice or noodles.

WESSEX CHICKEN

Serves 4

4 chicken portions
2 oz. plain flour
Oil for frying
3 medium-large carrots, chopped
2 small onions, chopped

1 pint sweet cider
2 egg yolks
½ pint cream
½ lb. mushrooms
2 oz. butter

Coat chicken pieces with flour and fry in oil until nicely browned. Add carrots and onions, pour over the cider and cook gently for 30–40 minutes.

Remove chicken and set aside. Sieve or blend what remains in the pan, and heat to reduce to about half the quantity.

Mix the egg yolks with the cream and blend with the sauce. Season to taste.

Place chicken in shallow dish and cover with sauce.

Cook the mushrooms in the butter for about 5 minutes and sprinkle over the top.

Serve garnished with fresh chopped parsley.

WEST AFRICAN PEANUT CHICKEN

Serves 4

1 chicken
Sauce:
3 tablespoons peanut butter
½ pint water
1 onion, chopped

1 green pepper, chopped
¼ teaspoon chilli powder
Salt and pepper

Place chicken in casserole. Pre-heat oven to 350°F/180°C/Gas Mark 4.

Make sauce: Put peanut butter in a pan on low heat and gradually add the water. Bring slowly to the boil. Add rest of ingredients and simmer 2–3 minutes to thicken.

Pour sauce over chicken, and cook for 1 ½ hours, until chicken is well-done.

Take chicken out of dish, remove meat from bones and stir into sauce.

Serve from casserole with boiled rice and such side dishes as chopped tomatoes, peppers, cucumber, hard-boiled eggs, chutney, salted peanuts, desiccated coconut.

MEAT

BEEF

AFRICAN STEW OR OFE OFEFA

Serves 4

1 lb. stewing beef
¼ lb. onions, chopped
Oil for frying
1 level teaspoon curry powder
Pinch chilli powder

Good handful spinach leaves
Medium tin tomatoes
1 level tablespoon tomato purée
Salt and pepper

Simmer beef in ½ pint water until tender. Remove meat. Reserve liquid.
Sauté onions in oil, add meat cut into small pieces, and curry and chilli
  powder. Cook for 5 minutes.
Add spinach and tomatoes and simmer gently for 10 minutes.
Add meat liquor and tomato purée and cook gently for at least an hour
  – the longer the better.
Season to taste.

Serve with rice.

BATTALION BEEF BAKE

Serves 4

Lower layer:
  ½ lb. onions, sliced
  ½ clove garlic, crushed
  ¾ lb. piece of bacon,
    cut in 1½ in. cubes
  1¼ lb. lean minced beef
  1 small orange
  8 oz. tin tomatoes
  Salt and pepper
  Bay leaf

  ¼ teaspoon Worcester sauce
Upper layer:
  2 lb. potatoes
Sauce:
  1 oz. margarine
  1 oz. plain flour
  12 fl. oz. milk
  ½ level teaspoon made mustard
  2 oz. Cheddar cheese, grated
  1 tablespoon Parmesan cheese

36

Pre-heat oven to 425°F/220°C/Gas Mark 7.
Fry onion and garlic lightly, add bacon and cook for 10 minutes.
Stir in mince and cook for 10 minutes more.
Pare orange rind into julienne strips, boil 5 minutes, drain.
Add peel, orange juice, tomatoes and seasoning to meat mixture,
    simmer for 45 minutes and turn into 3-pint casserole.
Meanwhile, slice and cook potatoes. Layer them over the meat.
Make the cheese sauce (for method see page 9, adding cheese after
    sauce has come to the boil), and spoon it over the dish.
Sprinkle top with Parmesan.
Bake 45 minutes.

BEEF LINDSTROM

Serves 6

1½ lb. lean minced beef	8 oz. cup finely diced cooked potatoes
1 egg	8 oz. cup finely diced cooked beetroot
Salt and pepper	Butter for frying
1 tablespoon finely chopped onion	

Combine meat with beaten egg, salt and pepper and mix thoroughly.
Carefully mix in rest of ingredients.
Shape into six large flat patties. Melt some butter in a large heavy skillet.
    When butter turns golden brown, add patties. Fry until golden
    brown, turn and fry other side until done to your liking.

Can be served topped with fried eggs.

ECONOMICAL BEEF STROGANOFF

Serves 4

1½ lb. braising steak	2 tablespoons tomato purée
2 medium onions, chopped	¾ pint chicken stock
6 oz. mushrooms, chopped	Salt and finely ground black pepper
Oil for frying	Small carton soured cream
1 tablespoon plain flour	(or fromage frais)

Cut meat into narrow strips. Heat oil in pan and fry meat quickly.
    Remove from pan.
Fry onions and then add mushrooms.

Return meat to pan and mix with onions and mushrooms.
Stir in flour and cook for 2 minutes. Stir in tomato purée and seasoning
and gradually add chicken stock. Cook gently for 1¼ hours.
Just before serving, stir in small carton of soured cream or fromage frais.

Serve with brown rice and a green salad.

MELLOW BEEF WITH PRUNES

Serves 12

2 lb. braising steak
Salt and pepper
3 oz. fat for frying
12 oz. onions, peeled and sliced in rings
8 oz. pitted prunes
2 teaspoons juniper berries, crushed coarsely
3–4 blades mace
1 lemon, including coarsely grated rind
5–6 teaspoons anchovy essence
½ pint stout
½ pint cream
1¼–1½ lb. shell- or bow-shaped pasta

Cut beef into 1–2 in. cubes, season and leave for an hour or more at
room temperature.
Heat 2 oz. fat in pan and fry beef over a high heat, stirring to brown it all
over (probably in 2–3 panfuls) and remove it to a casserole.
Heat the remaining 1 oz. fat in the pan and fry the onions over a
moderate heat until softened. Stir into the beef with the prunes,
juniper berries, mace and grated lemon rind.
Pre-heat the oven to 475°F/250°C/Gas Mark 9.
Mix the anchovy essence in a bowl with the stout, add some salt and
pepper and pour over the beef. Cover the casserole and place in the
centre of the oven for 20–25 minutes, until beginning to bubble.
Lower heat to 275°F/130°C/Gas Mark 1 and cook for 2¼–2½ hours, until
meat is tender.
Towards the end of this time, cook the pasta.
When the casserole is ready, pour in the cream and gradually stir in the
lemon juice to thicken. Spread the cooked pasta in the bottom of a
large open serving dish and spoon the beef and juices over the top.

Decorate with chopped parsley.

MINCED BEEF CASSEROLE

Serves 4–6

1 lb. minced beef
2 onions, chopped
2 sticks celery, chopped
8 oz. pasta
Tin condensed tomato soup
Tin condensed mushroom soup
6 oz. mushrooms
Salt and pepper
1 teaspoon Worcester sauce

Topping:
Crisps or grated cheese

Pre-heat oven to 350°F/180°C/Gas Mark 4.
Lightly fry mince, onions and celery.
Cook the pasta.
Combine all ingredients and put into buttered casserole.
Sprinkle topping over. Bake for 1 hour.

SAVOURY RICE WITH MINCED BEEF

Serves 5–6

2 medium onions, chopped
1 small green pepper, chopped
1 clove garlic, crushed
1 lb. minced beef
2 tablespoons plain flour
1 level teaspoon pepper
2 teaspoons sugar
3 cups water
6 oz. Patna rice, washed

1 oz. fat for frying
2 teaspoons salt
1 teaspoon chilli powder
2 × 14 oz. tins tomatoes
1 bay leaf
Topping:
4 oz. fresh breadcrumbs
A little margarine

Pre-heat oven to 350°F/180°C/Gas Mark 4.
Fry onions, pepper and garlic until cooked. Remove from pan.
Fry mince until browned.
Add flour and cook 1–2 minutes.
Add all other ingredients and simmer for 30 minutes, stirring
    occasionally. Remove from heat and remove bay leaf.
Turn into casserole, top with breadcrumbs and dot with margarine.
Bake for 40 minutes.

Serve with green salad.

SOMERSET BEEF CASSEROLE WITH DUMPLINGS

Serves 4

1 ½ lb. stewing beef
1 oz. plain flour, seasoned
1 oz. margarine
3 medium onions, chopped
4 sticks celery (or carrots), chopped
1 teaspoon fresh thyme (or rosemary)
   or ½ teaspoon dried
½ pint dry cider
½ pint beef stock
1 tablespoon black treacle
1 large cooking apple, peeled and sliced

Dumplings:
  4 oz. self-raising flour
  2 oz. beef suet
  Salt and pepper
1 red apple, sliced

Pre-heat oven to 400°F/200°/Gas Mark 6.
Toss meat in seasoned flour, and cook lightly in melted margarine on
   fairly low heat until browned and sealed.
Add onions and lightly cook for a few minutes. Keep heat low and
   continue to cook while preparing celery and cooking apple.
Remove pan from heat and add celery, apple, thyme, cider, stock and
   treacle.
Place pan on heat again, and when slightly thickened pour into
   casserole. Cover and cook for about 1¾ hours.
Make dumplings with flour, suet, seasoning and water. Do not make
   too wet. Roll into about eight small balls, coat in flour and add to
   casserole for 15–20 minutes, uncovered.
Place red apple slices between dumplings before serving.

SWISS STEAK

Serves 4

1½ lb. braising steak
2 tablespoons plain flour, seasoned
3 onions, thinly sliced
8 oz. mushrooms, sliced
1 green pepper, thinly sliced (optional)

1 carrot, chopped (optional)
14 oz. tin tomatoes (or 5 fresh
   tomatoes, peeled and sliced)
1 beef stock cube dissolved in
   ½ cup boiling water

Pre-heat oven to 325°F/160°C/Gas Mark 3.
Coat steak in flour and fry quickly to seal.
Place in casserole with the other ingredients and bake for a minimum of
1 ½ hours.

LAMB

'BARBECUED' LAMB CHOPS

Serves 6

2 lb. lamb chops, trimmed
Black pepper
2 tablespoons honey
2 tablespoons tomato ketchup
2 tablespoons soy sauce

2 tablespoons chopped garlic (or onion)
1 chicken stock cube
½ pint boiling water
1 tablespoon cornflour

Pre-heat oven to 450°F/230°C/Gas Mark 8.
Put chops in roasting tin, sprinkle with pepper and roast in centre of
oven for 5 minutes each side.
Meanwhile put honey, ketchup, soy sauce, garlic and stock cube in
heatproof bowl, pour on boiling water and stir until cube dissolves.
Pour over chops.
Turn oven down to 350°F/180°C/Gas Mark 4, and continue cooking
chops for another 30 minutes until tender.
Mix cornflour to a paste with water. Transfer roasting tin to top of
cooker and stir paste in, cooking until it thickens.

LAMB WITH A DIFFERENCE

Serves 2 generously

¾ lb. lean lamb, cubed
1 medium onion, sliced
1 small clove garlic, crushed
1 tablespoon plain flour
Salt and plenty of black pepper
½ teaspoon ground cumin
½ teaspoon ground allspice
2 oz. dried apricots, soaked in ½ pint water
1 tablespoon tomato purée
1 oz. whole blanched almonds

41

Pre-heat oven to 300°F/150°C/Gas Mark 2.
Brown lamb lightly, remove from pan. Place in bottom of casserole.
In same pan, sauté onion and garlic. When soft, add flour, seasoning
and spices and cook for 3 minutes.
Stir in apricot water and tomato purée.
Layer apricots on meat cubes with almonds, and pour contents of pan
over.
Cover and cook for 1½–2 hours, checking that it does not dry out in the
process.

PORK, BACON AND HAM

COURGETTES WITH HAM STUFFING AND CHEESE SAUCE

Serves 4

8 large courgettes

Stuffing:
3 tablespoons oil
Small onion, finely chopped
4 oz. ham, finely chopped
4 oz. fresh white breadcrumbs
2 tablespoons chopped fresh parsley
1 teaspoon dried thyme
1 tablespoon lemon juice
Salt and freshly ground black pepper
1 medium egg, beaten
Butter for greasing

Sauce:
1 oz. butter
1 oz. flour
10 fl. oz. milk
4 oz. Cheddar cheese, grated
Pinch nutmeg
Salt and freshly ground black
pepper

Pre-heat the oven to 375°F/190°C/Gas Mark 5.
Hollow out centre of courgettes by pushing an apple-corer into each
end. Boil them in salted water for 10 minutes to blanch, drain
thoroughly and pat dry.
Make stuffing: Fry the onion in the heated oil for 5 minutes, until soft.
Remove from heat and stir in all other ingredients, binding with the
egg.
Carefully stuff the courgettes, and arrange on a lightly buttered dish.
Cover with foil and bake for 30 minutes.
Meanwhile, make the sauce: Melt the butter, stir in the flour and cook

42

over a moderate heat for 2 minutes. Remove from heat, add milk gradually, return to heat, stirring until thick and smooth. Add the cheese, nutmeg and seasoning. Stir until the cheese has melted.

To serve, dish the courgettes on to four plates and pour the sauce over each.

ORIENTAL PORK

Serves 4

4 lean pork chops
1 medium onion, chopped
½ pint chicken stock
2 tablespoons vinegar
1 oz. tomato purée
1 ½ oz. peanuts, roughly chopped
1 small red or green pepper, sliced in rings

1 teaspoon soy sauce
2 teaspoons lemon juice
2 teaspoons sugar
1 teaspoon cornflour

Pre-heat oven to 300°F/150°C/Gas Mark 2.
Fry chops till brown then put in a casserole.
Fry onion in same fat.
Apart from the peanuts and pepper, mix all other ingredients together, add to onion and bring to the boil, stirring all the time. Pour this sauce over the chops.
Add the peanuts and arrange the pepper over the top. Cover and cook for 1 hour.

Serve with boiled rice or potatoes.

POSH BUBBLE AND SQUEAK

Onion, sliced
Bacon, rind removed, chopped
Left-over cooked cabbage (and carrots, etc.)
Left-over cooked potatoes, mashed

Fry onion and bacon until soft.
Add cabbage and fry for 2–3 minutes. Remove from pan and mix with potato.
Put more oil in pan and fry mixture until browned on bottom.

Serve with fried eggs.

SPICED CIDER BACON BAKE

Serves 4

4 bacon chops (or thick collar rashers)
4 oz. demerara sugar
½ teaspoon dry mustard
¼ teaspoon nutmeg
¼ teaspoon cinnamon

1 tablespoon cornflour
4 oz. mushrooms, sliced
4 slices pineapple
¼ pint dry cider
6 oz. American long-grain rice

Pre-heat oven to 350°F/180°C/Gas Mark 4.
Remove rind from chops and place in a shallow ovenproof dish.
Mix together the sugar, mustard, spices and cornflour and sprinkle over
the chops. Add the mushrooms and pineapple and pour over the
cider to cover.
Bake for 20–30 minutes.
Cook the rice. Make a bed of the cooked rice and serve the chops and
sauce on top.

SWEET AND SOUR PORK

Serves 6

6 pork chops
3 teaspoons soft brown (or demerara) sugar
4 teaspoons dry mustard
Salt and pepper
2 desertspoons lemon juice
14 oz. tin tomatoes
4 stuffed olives, sliced
4 gherkins, sliced

Pre-heat oven to 350°F/180°C/Gas Mark 4.
Put chops in greased baking dish.
Mix sugar and mustard and spread over chops. Season and sprinkle
with lemon juice. Pour tomatoes over and put olives and gherkins on
top.
Bake for 40–45 minutes.

SWEET AND SOUR PORK AND VEGETABLES

Serves 2

4 oz. rice
8 oz. raw lean pork, in thin strips
Oil for frying
1 medium onion, thinly sliced
2 carrots, thinly sliced
½ green pepper, sliced

Sauce:
1 level tablespoon cornflour
½ pint stock (or water)
3 level tablespoons sugar
1 level tablespoon tomato purée
2 level tablespoons soy sauce
1 level tablespoon vinegar
Pinch grated root ginger (optional)

Cook the rice and keep it warm.
Make the sauce: Blend cornflour with the stock, then mix with all the other ingredients.
Heat oil in a large pan or wok, and fry the meat for 2 minutes on very high heat, stirring all the time.
Add the chopped vegetables and fry for 1 minute, again stirring all the time.
Add sauce, stirring continuously. When thick and bubbling, simmer for a further minute.
Serve immediately on a bed of rice.

Cooked chicken or turkey can be used instead of pork.

OFFAL
LIVER IN BATTER

Serves 2

½ lb. liver (lamb's or pig's), cut into small thin portions
Batter:
2 tablespoons plain wholemeal flour
Pinch of salt
Cold water

Prepare a pan of boiling vegetable oil.
Make up batter.
Dip each portion of liver in batter and fry until golden brown.
Serve hot with vegetables.

VEGETABLES

BRAISED CELERY WITH CARROTS AND ONIONS

Serves 2

2 large sticks celery
4 oz. carrots
1 oz. butter
1 medium onion, chopped
½ teaspoon celery seeds
  (optional)

4 fl. oz. water
Salt and freshly ground black
  pepper
Fresh chopped parsley

Trim the celery stalks, cut in half lengthways, then cut the lengths into
  2 in. pieces.
The carrots should be cut into strips about the size of very small chips.
In a medium saucepan (which has a tight-fitting lid) melt the butter, stir
  in the onion and cook for a minute or two before adding the carrot
  and celery. Toss around in the hot butter until they are tinged golden
  at the edges (3–4 minutes).
Sprinkle in the celery seeds then pour in the water, season, cover (with
  the tight-fitting lid), turn the heat down and simmer for about 5
  minutes, until tender. Remove the lid and boil briskly until the liquid
  has reduced to about a tablespoon.
Sprinkle with parsley before serving.

CAULIFLOWER, MUSHROOM AND OAT CASSEROLE

Serves 4 as a supper dish

1 medium cauliflower, cut into
  even-sized florets
2 tablespoons plain flour
10 fl. oz. yogurt (or soured
  cream)
1 teaspoon mild mustard

6 oz. mature cheese, grated
8 oz. button mushrooms
1 oz. butter
4 oz. rolled oats
2 oz. walnuts, coarsely
  chopped

46

Pre-heat the oven to 400°F/200°C/Gas Mark 6.

Drop the florets into a saucepan containing about 1½ in. boiling salted water and cook for about 7 minutes, until just tender. Drain well.

Meanwhile, put the flour into a small bowl and blend with a little of the yogurt. Gradually stir in the remaining yogurt, mustard and half the cheese. Season to taste.

Mix in the cauliflower and mushrooms, turning gently so that they become coated. Pour into a shallow ovenproof dish.

Using a fork, mix the butter with the oats, then add the rest of the cheese and the walnuts to make a crumbly mixture.

Sprinkle over the cauliflower and mushrooms and bake for 40 minutes until the top is golden-brown and crisp.

COLD CURRY SAUCE

2 oz. clear honey
½ oz. curry powder
2 oz. fruit chutney
2 ½ fl. oz. white wine
¼ pint double cream
½ pint mayonnaise

Simmer honey and curry powder in a pan for 10 minutes. Add chutney and wine and simmer for 5 minutes. Leave to cool.

Whip cream and fold in mayonnaise. Just before serving, put two mixtures together and fold in chosen cold meat or fish.

COURGETTES WITH FRESH LIME

Serves 4–6

1 lb. courgettes
1 lime
1 oz. butter

Grate courgettes finely in strips and mix with lime rind and juice. Leave to marinate for some hours.

Toss in heated butter for about 4 minutes immediately before serving.

GREEN RICE

Serves 4

5 oz. Cheddar cheese, grated
8 fl. oz. milk
2½ oz. butter
2 eggs, beaten

1 clove garlic, crushed (optional)
7 oz. rice, cooked
1 cup chopped parsley
Salt and pepper

Pre-heat oven to 350°F/180°C/Gas Mark 4.
Mix together cheese, milk and butter and melt in a saucepan.
When melted, mix with eggs, garlic, rice and parsley. Season to taste.
Put into a greased casserole dish and bake for 30 minutes or until the top
is a light golden brown. Serve hot.

HERBED CARROTS

Serves 4

1 lb. new carrots
1 oz. butter
2 tablespoons chicken stock
1 clove garlic, finely chopped
1 medium onion, finely
chopped

1 tablespoon finely chopped
parsley
2 tablespoons finely chopped
rosemary
Salt and pepper

Cut carrots diagonally into thin slices.
Heat butter in saucepan and add all ingredients. Cover and cook over
low heat for 15–20 minutes, until carrots are barely tender.

HONEYED PARSNIPS

Serves 4

1½ lb. parsnips, peeled and
quartered
1 oz. butter
2 tablespoons orange juice
1 tablespoons lemon juice
2 tablespoons clear honey

Cook parsnips in boiling salted water for 10–15 minutes, until barely
    tender. Drain thoroughly.
In a heavy-bottomed saucepan heat together the butter, juices and
    honey. When blended, add the parsnips.
Cook over low heat for 5–10 minutes, turning the parsnips gently now
    and then until they are coated with the glaze.
Serve hot.

LAYERED POTATOES
WITH SOURED CREAM

Serves 2

12 oz. potatoes, thinly sliced
1 small onion, finely chopped
4 tablespoons soured cream
Salt and pepper

1½ oz. butter
4 tablespoons milk
Chopped chives

Pre-heat oven to 375°F/190°C/Gas Mark 5.
Line the base of a greased 1 pint ovenproof dish with potato slices. Add
    a little of the onion and soured cream. Sprinkle liberally with salt and
    pepper. Repeat the layers until all the ingredients have been used up,
    finishing with potato.
Melt 1 oz. butter in a saucepan, stir in the milk and pour over the
    potatoes. Dot the remaining butter on top.
Cover and cook for 45 minutes.
Uncover and cook for a further 20 minutes, until the potatoes are
    golden-brown.
Sprinkle with chives just before serving.

MEDITERRANEAN VEGETABLES

Serves 2

1 small aubergine, thinly sliced
Salt
1½ tablespoons oil
1 small onion, sliced
1 small clove garlic, crushed
1 celery stick, chopped
½ green pepper, chopped

2 tomatoes, skinned and
    chopped
2 tablespoons water
½ teaspoon dried oregano
½ teaspoon dried basil
Salt and pepper to taste

49

Sprinkle aubergine slices with salt and leave in colander for 30 minutes. Rinse and pat dry with kitchen towel.

Heat oil in saucepan and cook all the vegetables except the tomatoes, stirring until they are all coated in oil. Cover and cook for 10 minutes.

Add the rest of the ingredients, bring to the boil, cover and simmer for 30 minutes.

Serve hot or cold, sprinkled with parsley.

MÉLANGE BOURGUIGNON

Serves 6–8 and takes 3 days to prepare

Marinade:

¾ pint red wine	12 juniper berries, crushed
1 teaspoon sea salt	1 teaspoon mustard powder
12 whole peppercorns, crushed	4 tablespoons brandy
	Sprig fresh rosemary

Mélange:

4 oz. dried apricots	2 tablespoons olive oil
4 oz. dried chickpeas	1 pint vegetable stock
4 oz. dried chestnuts	1 tablespoon paprika
Large aubergine	1 lemon, zest and juice
2 large onions	1 tablespoon brown sugar
2 large carrots	Black pepper and sea salt to
10 cloves garlic	taste

First day: Prepare marinade. Put apricots, chickpeas and chestnuts to soak overnight, separately, in cold water.

Second day: Boil chickpeas in plenty of water for 2 hours or in pressure cooker. Drain and add to marinade. Boil chestnuts 30 minutes and add to marinade, removing remnants of skin. Simmer apricots for 15 minutes and add to marinade.

Third day: Chop aubergines into cubes, sprinkle with salt and leave 2 hours. Rinse, drain and pat dry. Add to marinade. Slice onions, carrots and garlic and cook for a few moments in the heated oil in a thick-bottomed saucepan. Add to marinade with the stock. Bring to the boil and simmer for 1 ½ hours. Remove from the heat and extract all the vegetables, keeping them warm. Return pan to the heat and add the paprika, lemon and sugar. Boil to reduce to about ½ pint of thick sticky sauce. Return vegetables and mix carefully. Season and serve.

NOODLES WITH WALNUTS

Serves 6–8

1½ lb. ribbon noodles
4 oz. butter
3 oz. shelled walnuts, coarsely
   chopped

1 oz. fresh white breadcrumbs
Salt and ground black pepper

Cook noodles in boiling salted water until tender but firm.
Drain thoroughly and transfer to deep, heated serving dish and keep
   hot.
Meanwhile, melt the butter in a small frying pan and sauté the walnuts
   and breadcrumbs until crisp and golden.
Stir this mixture into the noodles, season to taste and mix again gently
   before serving.

SPICED CABBAGE WITH APPLE

Serves 6

1 large firm green cabbage
1 lb. apples (sharp eating or
   mild cooking)
¼ pint dry cider
5 tablespoons water

3 oz. unsalted butter
Salt and pepper
Pinch of nutmeg
1 clove garlic, crushed

Trim the cabbage and remove part of the stalk. Blanch it whole in a large
   pan of boiling salted water for 10 minutes after the water has
   returned to the boil. Drain it and let it cool a little. Quarter and slice
   it, discarding any woody parts.
Peel, quarter and core the apples.
Mix together all the ingredients except the butter. Bring the liquid to
   boiling point, cover and leave to simmer for 45 minutes, stirring from
   time to time. If it is too wet, remove the lid and raise the heat to
   evaporate the excess liquid.
Check the seasoning, stir in the butter in pieces and serve.

SAVOURY SNACKS

BACON SAVOURY

Serves 4

8 slices of bacon with rind
   trimmed off
6 oz. packet of sage and onion
   stuffing
1 egg, beaten
Oil (or lard) for cooking

Pre-heat oven to 350°F/180°C/Gas Mark 4.
Mix egg with stuffing, adding a little hot water if necessary.
Spread each slice of bacon with stuffing mix and roll up.
Bake for 25–30 minutes.

Thinly sliced potatoes may be cooked alongside.

CHEESE CRISPS

1 cup grated Cheddar cheese
1 cup crushed potato crisps
2 oz. butter
2 oz. plain flour
Pinch cayenne pepper
1 teaspoon made mustard

Pre-heat oven to 350°F/180°C/Gas Mark 4.
Mix everything together. Place teaspoonfuls on baking tray and press
   lightly with spoon.
Bake 12 minutes until golden.
Cool on tray.

CHEESE NIBBLES

Makes approx. 30

4 oz. plain flour
2 oz. margarine
2 oz. cheese, grated
Sesame seeds

Salt
Cayenne pepper
1 egg, beaten
Small amount water

Rub fat into flour, add cheese, a few sesame seeds and seasoning. Stir in
   egg and as much water as is needed to bind. Leave ½ hour.
Pre-heat oven to 425°F/220°C/Gas Mark 7.
Roll on floured board and scatter more sesame seeds over. Cut into
   shapes.
Bake for 12–15 minutes.

CHEESE STRAWS

Makes approx. 30

3 oz. mature cheese, grated
3 oz. butter (or margarine)

4 oz. plain flour
Pinch paprika (or cayenne pepper)

Cream fat and cheese together and blend in the flour and paprika. Roll
   into a ball and keep in fridge overnight.
Roll out, cut into straws and bake at 350°F/180°C/Gas Mark 4 for 10–15
   minutes.

CHICKEN QUICHE

Serves 4–6

8 oz. shortcrust pastry
1 large onion, chopped
3 oz. bacon, chopped
6 oz. cooked chicken, chopped
3 eggs
1 tin condensed mushroom
   soup
Salt and pepper
6 oz. cheese, grated (optional)

Topping:
   Small amount cheese, grated

Pre-heat oven to 375°F/190°C/Gas Mark 5.
Line a greased 9 in. flan tin with shortcrust pastry. (For method see page 9.)
Fry onion and bacon until onion is soft, and drain well.
Mix all ingredients together and pour into flan case.
Sprinkle with cheese and bake for 45 minutes, until set and golden brown.

Serve hot or cold.

FRENCH ONION LOAF

1 packet French onion soup (for making 1½ pints)
½ pint milk
6 oz. margarine

14 oz. self-raising flour
1 teaspoon baking powder
2 eggs
At least 2 oz. cheese (grated)

Pre-heat oven to 350°F/180°C/Gas Mark 4.
Mix soup powder with milk and leave for 10 minutes.
Mix remaining ingredients together and add soup mixture. Mix well and pour into greased 2 lb. loaf tin.
Bake for 1½ hours.

HERBY SAUSAGE PLAIT

Serves 6

8 oz. flaky or puff pastry (frozen may be used for convenience)
1 lb. sausagemeat

2 oz. parsley, thyme and lemon stuffing mix
1 small onion, finely chopped
1 egg, beaten, to glaze

Pre-heat oven to 400°F/200°C/Gas Mark 6.
Roll out pastry thinly, forming an oblong approx. 10 in. × 8 in. Mark three equal sections lengthways.
Make stuffing as directed on packet and mix with sausagemeat and onion. Spread down middle section of pastry, leaving a 1 in. space at top and bottom.
Using sharp knife, cut diagonal (downward-pointing) ½ in. strips each

side of filling. Starting at top, take strips from alternating sides and lay across filling to make the plait, and tuck in ends to neaten. Brush with egg and bake for 30 minutes.

PIZZA TOAST

Serves 1

Thick slice of bread
1 clove garlic, cut in half
Tomato purée
Pinch mixed herbs or oregano
1 oz. cheese, grated
1 slice ham, chopped (optional)

Lightly toast bread on both sides.
Rub garlic on toast.
Spread thinly with tomato purée and sprinkle with herbs, ham and
  cheese.
Grill until cheese melts and bubbles.

SANDCASTLES

(For children's lunch)

Potatoes
Cheddar cheese, grated
Cabbage, shredded and blanched in boiling water for 8 minutes, or until
  tender.
Prawns, peeled

Boil, drain and mash potatoes.
Working as quickly as possible, so that they are served warm, form the
  potato into pyramid shapes (about 2 tablespoons per pyramid),
  sprinkle them with cheese ('sand') and decorate them with cabbage
  ('seaweed') and a few prawns.

N.B. The quantities required for this recipe depend on the number and size of the children being served!

SAUSAGE PLAIT

Serves 4

Pastry:
5 oz. hard margarine, softened

2 tablespoons water
8 oz. plain flour, sieved

Filling:
½lb sausage meat
1 medium onion, finely chopped
2 oz. mushrooms, chopped
1 large tomato, sliced

½ teaspoon dried rosemary (or mixed herbs)
1 egg, beaten, (or milk) to glaze

Make pastry: Put margarine, water and 4 tablespoons flour in mixing bowl. Cream together with fork until well mixed (½ minute). Stir in remaining flour to form firm dough. Knead lightly on floured board. Roll out thinly to make approx. 11 in. square.

Pre-heat oven to 375°F/190°C/Gas Mark 5.

Mix all filling ingredients together. Place in strip 3 in. wide down centre of pastry. Using sharp knife, cut diagonal (downward-pointing) ½ in. strips each side of filling. Starting at top, take strips from alternating sides and lay across filling to make the plait. Tuck in ends to neaten. Transfer to baking sheet. Brush with egg and bake on middle shelf for 45–55 minutes.

Serve hot or cold, with tomato sauce.

SAVOURY DORSET TEA-BREAD

4 oz. bacon, finely chopped
2 apples, peeled, cored and chopped
1 small onion, grated
½ lb. self-raising flour

Salt and pepper
1 oz. lard
1 egg
5 tablespoons milk

Pre-heat oven to 375°F/190°C/Gas Mark 5.

Fry bacon, apple and onion. Allow to cool.

Sift flour, salt and pepper, and rub in lard until mixture resembles fine breadcrumbs. Add bacon mixture.

Beat together egg and milk and stir into flour. Spoon into greased 1 lb. loaf tin and bake for 40 minutes.

Serve sliced and buttered.

SAVOURY FLAPJACKS

Makes approx. 20

4 oz. margarine
8 oz. rolled oats
3 oz. cheese, grated
Small amount of grated onion (optional)
Salt and pepper
½ teaspoon dry mustard
1 large egg

Pre-heat oven to 400°F/200°C/Gas Mark 6.
Cream margarine until soft, and mix in all other ingredients.
Press into well-greased tin and cook for 30 minutes.
Cut into squares when cold.

SPINACH AND COTTAGE CHEESE QUICHE

Serves 4–6

6 oz. shortcrust pastry
8 oz. packet frozen chopped spinach, thawed
8 oz. cottage cheese
3 eggs, beaten
1 oz. Parmesan cheese
Salt and pepper
4 tablespoons thin cream (or milk)

Make pastry (for method see page 9).
Line greased quiche tin with pastry and put in fridge to rest.
Pre-heat oven to 375°F/190°C/Gas Mark 5.
Mix together all ingredients and pour into pastry case.
Bake in centre of oven for 40–45 minutes, until firm.

TOMATO PIE

Serves 4

8 oz. shortcrust pastry
4 oz. breadcrumbs
2 oz. cheese, grated

1 lb. tomatoes, pulped
1 onion, sliced
Salt and pepper

Pre-heat oven to 350°F/180°C/Gas Mark 4.
Make the pastry (for method see page 9).
Line a 9 in. greased pie dish with the pastry.
Mix the breadcrumbs with the cheese, and put half aside for the
    topping. Mix the rest with the other ingredients and put in the pie
    dish. Sprinkle on the topping, dot with margarine or butter and bake
    for 30 minutes.

VEGETABLE FLAN

Serves 4

6 oz. shortcrust pastry
1 medium onion, chopped
3 medium carrots, chopped
4 oz. mushrooms, sliced
1 oz. butter (or margarine)
2 eggs
¼ pint milk
4 oz. cheese, grated

Make pastry (for method see page 9).
Line a greased 7 in. or 8 in. flan dish with pastry.
Pre-heat oven to 385°F/195°C/Gas Mark 5½.
Toss vegetables in heated butter for a few minutes. Allow to cool.
Beat eggs into milk and add 3 oz. of the grated cheese. Mix with the
    vegetables and pour into the flan dish. Sprinkle with the rest of the
    cheese.
Bake in centre of oven for 30 minutes.
Lower heat to 335°F/170°C/Gas Mark 3½ and bake for a further 15
    minutes.

Serve hot or cold.

SALADS

BEAN SALAD

Serves 10–12

15 oz. tin kidney beans
15 oz. tin green cut beans
15 oz. tin yellow wax beans (or
  butter beans)
1 small onion, finely chopped
½ small green pepper, finely
  chopped

2–3 tablespoons vegetable oil
2 tablespoons white wine
  vinegar
1 dessertspoon caster sugar
Salt and pepper

Drain and rinse beans, and put in large bowl.
Add all other ingredients and mix. Leave in fridge overnight to
  marinate.

BEAN SPROUT SALAD

Serves 2

1 tablespoon French dressing
1 tablespoon yogurt
Salt and pepper
4 oz. fresh bean sprouts
1 stick celery, chopped

1 carrot, grated
1 in. piece of cucumber, cut in
  strips
3 tablespoons raisins

Combine the French dressing with the yogurt and season to taste.
Mix well with all the other ingredients.

CARROT SALAD

Serves 4–6

1 lb. carrots, finely grated
4 oz. raisins
Dressing:
  3 tablespoons natural yogurt

Grated rind and juice of large orange
Good pinch mixed herbs
1 tablespoon salad oil
Salt and pepper

59

Mix dressing ingredients together, pour over carrots and raisins and mix well.

This can be left overnight as it helps to plump up the raisins.

CHINESE CABBAGE, CARROT AND BEAN SPROUT SALAD

Serves 4

½ head Chinese cabbage,
  shredded
4 oz. bean sprouts
4 oz. carrots, coarsely grated
Dressing:
  4 tablespoons oil
  Juice of a lemon
  1 tablespoon soy sauce
  1 teaspoon clear honey
  1 clove garlic, crushed
  ½ teaspoon ground ginger
2 tablespoons sesame seeds

Combine cabbage, bean sprouts and carrots.
Beat together the dressing ingredients and stir into the salad.
Toast the sesame seeds in a frying pan over a moderate heat until they are brown, stirring all the time. Scatter over the salad and serve while seeds are still warm.

CURRIED MUSHROOMS

Serves 4

5 oz. yogurt
2 tablespoons chutney
6 tablespoons salad cream

1 teaspoon curry powder
Salt and pepper
12 oz. raw mushrooms, sliced

Mix all ingredients and chill for 2 hours.

PEANUT COLESLAW

Serves 4–6

1 lb. green or white cabbage,
  finely shredded
3 large carrots, coarsely grated
2 eating apples, quartered,
  cored and thinly sliced
2 oz. salted peanuts

Dressing:
8 fl. oz. mayonnaise
2 teaspoons French mustard
1 tablespoon lemon juice
Salt and pepper to taste

Mix together the main ingredients.
Make the dressing and pour it over. Mix well.
Chill before serving.

PEAR AND WATERCRESS SALAD

Serves 4

1 dessert pear
1 bunch watercress
½ stick celery, cut into julienne
  strips

Dressing:
1 tablespoon wine vinegar
1 teaspoon French mustard
Pinch salt
Ground black pepper
4 tablespoons oil

Wash watercress and wrap in a damp tea towel.
Make dressing: Combine all ingredients except oil, then beat in the oil
  with a whisk until dressing thickens.
Just before serving, quarter and core the pear. Cut each quarter into six
  slices and toss everything together in a salad bowl. Serve
  immediately.

RED CABBAGE AND
PINEAPPLE SLAW

Serves 4–6

8 oz. tin pineapple rings
2 tablespoons French dressing
Salt and freshly ground black pepper

6 spring onions, chopped
1 oz. sultanas
6 oz. red cabbage, shredded

61

Reserving 1 tablespoon of the syrup, drain and chop the pineapple rings and put them in a bowl.

Mix the tablespoon of pineapple syrup with the dressing, season well and add to the pineapple with all the other ingredients. Mix well.

REFRIGERATOR COLESLAW

Serves 12

4–5 lb. white cabbage, thinly sliced
4 large carrots, finely chopped
1 bunch spring onions, finely chopped
6 tablespoons sugar

2 teaspoons dry mustard
1 teaspoon salt
1 cup white wine vinegar
1 cup vegetable oil
2 teaspoons celery seeds

Put cabbage, carrots and spring onions in mixing bowl and sprinkle over about 2 tablespoons sugar (this amount can be varied).

Mix 4 tablespoons sugar with the mustard and salt in a milk pan, and add the vinegar. Bring to the boil, stirring to dissolve the sugar.

Add the oil and the celery seeds and bring to the boil again. Pour over the salad while hot.

Leave to cool, cover and chill.

This salad will keep for several weeks in the fridge.

SLICED 'CUKES'

Serves 8

1 cup white wine vinegar
2 cups granulated sugar
7 cups sliced cucumber
2 cups sliced green peppers
1 cup very thinly sliced onion
1 tablespoon celery seeds
1 tablespoon salt

Stir vinegar and sugar well, add rest of ingredients. Stir again.

Keep in a covered plastic bowl or jar in the fridge, stirring every couple of days. It will keep for several months.

SUMMER SALAD

Serves 4
(This salad is best made the day before use.)

2 cups cooked rice
1 lb. tin apricots, drained and diced
1 small onion, chopped
½ cup seedless raisins (or sultanas)

1 large green pepper, deseeded and chopped
½ cup mayonnaise
2 tablespoons chutney
1 teaspoon curry powder
Salt

Put cooked rice into mixing bowl and add apricots, onion, raisins and green pepper.

Blend mayonnaise, chutney, curry powder and salt to taste, and pour over.

Toss lightly. Chill.

Garnish with lettuce leaves and tomato wedges.

TOSSED GREEN SALAD WITH AVOCADO

Serves 4

1 lettuce
1 bunch watercress
1 clove garlic, halved
2 tablespoons finely chopped chives
4 tablespoons oil

1 tablespoon wine vinegar
Salt and ground black pepper
1 avocado
Half a lemon (to squeeze over avocado)

Prepare lettuce and watercress.

Rub wooden salad bowl with the garlic, and arrange the lettuce and watercress.

Chop the garlic clove and combine with most of the chives. Sprinkle over the salad and dress with the oil and vinegar. Season to taste.

Just before serving, peel and slice the avocado and sprinkle the slices with lemon juice to prevent discolouration.

Toss the salad so that each leaf glistens, and place the avocado slices on the top.

WINTER SALAD

Serves 4

5 fl. oz. soured cream
6 tablespoons chopped walnuts
1 small clove of garlic, finely
　　chopped
Salt and freshly ground black
　　pepper
8 oz. white cabbage, finely
　　sliced
8 oz. red cabbage, finely sliced

Pour the soured cream into a large bowl, add the walnuts and garlic and
　　season to taste.
Add the cabbage and toss until evenly coated.

SWEETS AND PUDDINGS

APPLE SCONE PUDDING

Serves 4

8 oz. self-raising flour
2 oz. margarine (or butter)
3 oz. brown sugar

1 level teaspoon cinnamon
Milk to mix
1 lb. cooking apples

Pre-heat oven to 400°F/200°C/Gas Mark 6.

Rub fat into flour, stir in the cinnamon and half the sugar and mix into scone dough with milk.

Peel and slice the apples.

Press half the dough into greased 7 in. tin, and on top of this place the apples and the rest of the sugar. Press the rest of the dough on the top.

Bake for 30 minutes.

APPLE SNOWBALLS

Serves 4

4 cooking apples (Bramley if possible)
1 slice wholemeal bread
4 dessertspoons mincemeat (and/or dates)
½ oz. butter

Meringue:
2 egg whites
2 oz. caster sugar
1 oz. granulated sugar
Pinch cream of tartar

Pre-heat oven to 350°F/180°C/Gas Mark 4.

Core apples and score a line around their middles. Plug the bottom of each with a wedge of bread and put into a shallow ovenproof dish. Fill with mincemeat and top with a knob of butter.

Put 3 or 4 tablespoons water into dish and bake for 30–40 minutes in centre of oven. Apples must not be fully cooked at this stage, but cooked enough to enable their skins to be easily removed. Remove skins and turn oven down to 300°F/150°C/Gas Mark 2 if to be served hot, or to 225°F/110°C/Gas Mark ¼ if to be served cold.

Make meringue: Beat egg whites with cream of tartar until stiff and add caster sugar a little at a time, continuing beating, until firm and shiny. Fold in granulated sugar.

Coat each apple in meringue to look like a snowball.

If to be served hot, bake in centre of oven for about 20 minutes, until pale golden colour.

If to be served cold, bake for 1½–2 hours until dry and crisp.

BAKED BANANA CUSTARD

Serves 4

4 ripe bananas
5 tablespoons white sugar
¼ teaspoon nutmeg, plus one
    grating to sprinkle on top

Juice of a lemon
4 oz. white breadcrumbs
3 standard eggs
1 pint milk

Pre-heat oven to 350°F/180°C/Gas Mark 4.

Mash bananas. Add 2 tablespoons sugar, nutmeg and lemon juice and place in buttered baking dish. Cover with crumbs.

Beat the eggs with the rest of the sugar until golden and thick.

Heat milk until very hot, pour over the eggs and stir together. Pour over banana mixture, add grating of nutmeg and bake until custard is cooked.

Serve with thick cream.

BERRY CREAM

Serves 2

13½ oz. tin berries
(blackberries, raspberries, etc.)
2½ level teaspoons cornflour
5 fl. oz. soured cream
1 level tablespoon brown sugar

Strain the juice from the fruit.

Blend the cornflour with a little of the juice and heat the rest of the liquid. Stir the hot juice into the cornflour mixture, return to the pan and bring to the boil, stirring until it thickens.

Stir in the fruit, pour into a shallow ovenproof dish and cover the top with the soured cream. Sprinkle the brown sugar over the top and place under hot grill until the top is bubbly.

BLACK CHERRY MUDDLE

Serves 3

1 tin black cherry pie filling
¼ pint whipped cream
¼ pint yogurt

Topping:
Demerara sugar

Stir everything gently together and sprinkle with sugar. Refrigerate.

BOODLE

Serves 6

1 packet trifle sponges
2 lemons, grated rind and juice
4 oranges, grated rind and juice

3 oz. caster sugar
½ pint double cream, whipped

Line fairly shallow dish with sponges.

Mix rind and juice with sugar until dissolved and fold in cream. Pour over sponges and chill for several hours – it should firm up enough to serve.

CHANTILLY MERINGUE

Serves 4

2 digestive biscuits
½ oz. butter
3 oz. meringues

½ pint double cream
½ teaspoon vanilla essence
1 level tablespoon caster sugar

Crush biscuits. Melt butter and grease tin or mould. Line with crushed biscuits.

Lightly crush meringues. Whip cream with vanilla essence and sugar until it holds its shape, carefully fold in meringue with metal spoon and put in mould. Smooth top, put a plate on top and freeze for 3–4 hours.

Loosen sides with a knife and turn out.

Serve with a sharp fruit such as raspberries or strawberries.

CHOCOLATE MERINGUE DELIGHT

Serves 4

3 egg whites
6 oz. caster sugar
1 teaspoon lemon juice
Filling:

6 oz. cooking chocolate
4 oz. marshmallows
1 tablespoon milk

2 tablespoons sherry
Small carton double cream, whipped till stiff

Line two baking sheets with non-stick paper. Make approx. twenty meringues (for method see page 9).

Melt chocolate and marshmallows in the milk over hot water, stirring occasionally. Cool, stir in sherry and fold in cream.

Arrange a circular layer of meringues and pour some of the mixture over. Make the next layer smaller, and do the same. Continue in this way, finishing with one meringue in the centre at the top.

Can be decorated with chopped roasted almonds and more whipped cream.

DRUNKEN SPONGE

This is a filled fatless sponge made in a ring-shaped tin.

Fatless sponge:
3 large eggs
3 oz. caster sugar
3 oz. plain flour, sifted
½ teaspoon baking powder

Syrup:
4 tablespoons sugar
4 tablespoons water
¼ pint brandy (or rum)

Icing:

    6 oz. icing sugar, sifted
    Few drops hot water
    ½ pint double cream
    Small amount of white sugar
    Fresh strawberries (and/or
      other fruit) to decorate

Pre-heat oven to 350°F/180°C/Gas Mark 4.

Separate eggs, putting the whites in a large grease-free bowl. Add the sugar to the yolks in another bowl and whisk until the mixture is pale, fluffy and thick (about 5 minutes with an electric whisk).

Wash and dry whisk and beat whites until stiff, but not dry. Fold whites into egg mixture with metal spoon, alternating with sifted flour and baking powder, but starting and finishing with the egg whites.

Pour into a well-greased tin and bake for 20–25 minutes until firm to the touch and it has slightly shrunk away from the sides of the tin. Leave to cool for 3 minutes, then turn out on to a sheet of greaseproof paper sprinkled with caster sugar.

Make syrup: Dissolve the sugar in the water and boil for 5 minutes. Place sponge on a dish, make a few holes with a thin skewer and pour on the hot syrup and then the brandy.

Make icing: Place icing sugar in a bowl, add hot water a little at a time until icing is of a coating consistency. Ice the top of the sponge ring. Whip the cream, adding a little sugar, then pile in the centre of the ring and decorate with the strawberries.

FINNISH SOUR CAKE

Serves 6

4 oz. butter
5 oz. caster sugar
2 egg yolks

2 lemons (rind of 1 and juice of 2)
Large packet trifle sponges

Cream butter and sugar. Gradually beat in the egg yolks and lemon rind and juice.

Grease large basin (suitable for freezing). Cut sponges into 3 slices lengthways and put in a first layer of sponge. Alternate layers of mixture and sponge, ending with sponge. Press well down, cover with foil and put weight on top. Freeze.

When frozen remove from basin and serve.

FRUIT SWEET AND SOUR

Serves 6–8

2 lb. soft fruit
1 pint plain set yogurt

½ pint whipped cream
½ lb. approx. demerara sugar

Put fruit in a glass dish and mix lightly.
Mix yogurt with cream and spread over the fruit.
Over this spread about ½ in. of demerara sugar and refrigerate for at
    least 24 hours, by which time the sugar will be crisp.

FUDGE SAUCE

Makes approx. ½ pint

10 oz. brown sugar
3 fl. oz. milk
1 ½ level teaspoons sifted cocoa

1 teaspoon natural vanilla essence
1 teaspoon butter

Place all ingredients in a pan and bring to the boil slowly, stirring all the
    time. Leave to boil gently for approx. 8 minutes. To test, drop ½
    teaspoon of the mixture into cold water. It will form a soft ball if it is
    ready.

When poured over ice-cream it will form a thin toffee. It may be made in
    advance and reheated at the last minute.

GATEAU ST GEORGE

Serves 4

4 oz. chocolate polka dots
1 tablespoon water
1 egg, separated
2 oz. butter

Small amount strong black
    coffee (or rum)
1 small sponge flan
2 oz. sugar

Pre-heat oven to 300°F/150°/Gas Mark 2.
Melt chocolate with water in basin over hot water, and add egg yolk,
    butter and coffee. Pour into prepared flan case.
Beat egg white until stiff, fold in sugar and cover chocolate mixture.
    Bake for 30–45 minutes.

GREAT-GRANDMOTHER'S BREAD PUDDING

Serves 4

8 oz. stale bread
4 oz. hard margarine
3 oz. soft brown sugar

1 egg
4 oz. mixed dried fruit
½ teaspoon mixed spice (optional)

Pre-heat oven to 375°F/190°C/Gas Mark 5.

Soak the bread in cold water until soft, and then squeeze out as much water as possible.

Melt the margarine and mix well with all the other ingredients in a mixing bowl (an electric mixer or processor gives a finer texture).

Put into a lightly greased 9 in. × 1 ½ in. deep ovenproof dish and bake for 1 hour, until nicely browned.

Can be served hot (with custard) or cold.

HOT LEMON FLUFF

Serves 4

1 oz. margarine
1 oz. plain flour
¼ pint milk
2 tablespoons lemon juice
4 level tablespoons lemon curd
2 oz. sugar
3 large eggs, separated

Pre-heat oven to 350°F/180°C/Gas Mark 4 and grease a 1 ½–2 pint soufflé dish.

Melt margarine, stir in flour, and cook gently for ½ minute. Gradually stir in milk and bring to the boil. Reduce heat and simmer for 2 minutes.

Take off heat and stir in lemon juice, lemon curd and sugar.

Cool slightly then stir in egg yolks. Whisk the egg whites till stiff and stir one tablespoon into the sauce. Fold in the rest using a metal spoon.

Pour into soufflé dish and bake in the centre of the oven for 40–45 minutes until well risen, set and firm to the touch.

Serve at once.

LEMON DAINTY

Serves 4

6 oz. granulated sugar
1 level tablespoon plain flour
½ oz. butter

2 eggs, separated
1 lemon, grated rind and juice
Large cupful of milk

Pre-heat oven to 350°F/180°C/Gas Mark 4.

Beat together sugar, flour and butter. Add egg yolks and lemon. Beat until well blended then add milk and whisk until smooth.

Whisk egg whites and fold into mixture. Pour into ungreased baking dish. Stand this in a container of hot water and bake for 45 minutes in the middle of the oven.

This can wait for a while, in its dish of hot water in a low oven, before serving.

LEMON ICE-CREAM

Serves 8

½ pint double cream
½ lb. sugar

½ pint milk
2 large lemons, zest and juice

Beat together everything except the lemon juice, in a processor. Freeze for approx. 1 hour, then add the juice and beat again. Freeze.

Remove from the freezer about 10 minutes before using.

PINEAPPLE DELIGHT

Serves 4

15½ oz. tin pineapple in own juice
1 lemon jelly
Small carton yogurt

Melt jelly in ½ pint water. Add pineapple juice and make up to a pint with the yogurt.

Put pineapple in dish and pour jelly over. Leave to set.

PINEAPPLE DESSERT

Serves 4

15½ oz. tin pineapple in own
   juice
Sauce:
  1 oz. margarine
  1 oz. plain flour
  15 fl. oz. milk
  1 oz. sugar
2 eggs, separated
Small amount sugar

Strain pineapple, saving the juice, and put in ovenproof dish.
Make sauce (for method see page 9, adding sugar after the milk).
For meringue, whisk egg white till stiff, adding sugar to stiffen.
Add egg yolks and pineapple juice to sauce and stir over low heat until
  mixture resembles custard. Pour over pineapple and spread
  meringue over top.
Brown carefully in oven (300°F/150°C/Gas Mark 2), then chill.

Serve cold.

PINEAPPLE FROMAGE

Serves 4

½ cup sugar
2 eggs, separated
15½ oz. tin pineapple cubes in
  own juice

Juice of half lemon
½ oz. gelatine, soaked in 2
  tablespoons cold water
1 cup double cream, whipped

Beat egg yolks and sugar until fluffy.
Add lemon and pineapple juice and gelatine dissolved over hot water.
  Stir until thick.
Fold in stiffly beaten egg whites, whipped cream, and pineapple cubes.
Pour into a mould and refrigerate for 3 hours.

To serve, turn out and accompany with sweet biscuits.

RASPBERRY MOUSSE

Serves 4

1 raspberry jelly (or
    blackcurrant)
10 oz. whipping cream,
    whipped
½ lb. raspberries, mashed
Dash of lemon juice

Dissolve jelly in ½ pint water. When it begins to set, fold cream into it
    with fruit and lemon juice. Leave to set.

RUM AND SULTANA SYLLABUB

Serves 6

2 oz. sultanas
4 tablespoons rum
Juice of half a lemon
1½ oz. caster sugar
Pinch ground ginger
½ pint double cream, whisked

Put all ingredients except the cream into a bowl, mix together and leave
    until the sultanas have absorbed most of the liquid.
Fold in the cream and pour into individual dishes.

Decorate with crystallized ginger if desired.

SUMMER PUDDING*

Serves 8

Approx. 10 slices stale white
    bread (to line and cover 2 lb.
    loaf tin)
4 oz. granulated sugar
¼ pint water
1½ lb. soft summer fruit

Remove crusts from bread and cut slices in half.

Melt sugar in the water, add fruit and simmer gently for about 10 minutes. Soften the fruit but do not mash.

Line a 2 lb. loaf tin with a piece of cling-film large enough also to cover the top when filled.

Strain fruit and put juice in a shallow dish.

Dip the bread in the juice and, with the juicy sides next to the cling-film, lay 2–3 slices in the bottom of the tin, 1 each end and 2 each side.

Put in the fruit and cover with 2–3 dipped slices. Pour on any remaining juice. Cover with the cling-film and then foil, and put a weight (e.g. a bag of sugar on its side) on top.

Refrigerate overnight.

This can be frozen quite successfully.

VICTORIAN CHRISTMAS PUDDING

Makes approx. 4 × 1 pint puddings

1 lb. dried currants
1 lb. dried sultanas
1 lb. dried raisins
1 lb. dried prunes, soaked and stoned
½ lb. dried dates
1 medium carrot, peeled
1 medium potato, peeled
1 medium apple, peeled and cored
4 oz. mixed peel

1 teaspoon mixed spice
8 oz. plain flour
8 oz. beef suet
6 eggs (fresh or dried)
3 tablespoons black treacle
8 oz. demerara sugar
½ teaspoon nutmeg
8 oz. breadcrumbs
½ teaspoon salt
6 oz. dried milk (or ¼ pint fresh)

Clean and prepare all dried fruit, and put first eight ingredients through mincer.

Mix together all ingredients and leave overnight.

Put into basin(s) – 4 pints in all, approx. – and cover with greaseproof paper and cloth. Steam for 8 hours, adding more boiling water so that the pan does not dry out.

Keeps for up to 1 year. Steam for 1 hour to reheat before serving.

TEA-BREAD, BREAD AND SCONES

APPLE AND WALNUT TEA-BREAD

Makes two 1 lb. loaves

Large cooking apple, peeled,
  cored and chopped
4 oz. raisins
2 oz. chopped walnuts
4 oz. brown sugar
4 oz. soft margarine

2 eggs
1 tablespoon clear honey
6 oz. self-raising flour
2 oz. wholemeal flour
Pinch mixed spice
Pinch salt

Pre-heat oven to 350°F/180°C/Gas Mark 4.
Use two 1 lb. loaf tins, lined with greased greaseproof paper.
Put all ingredients in mixing bowl and beat for 2 minutes by hand or
  with an electric mixer.
Pour into the tins and bake for 1 hour.
Reduce heat to 325°F/160°C/Gas Mark 3 and cook for a further 20–30
  minutes, testing with a skewer to see if it is ready.
Turn on to a wire rack to cool.

APPLE, WALNUT AND SULTANA TEA-BREAD

Makes one 2 lb. loaf

4 oz. soft margarine
4 oz. caster sugar
3 small (or 2 large) eggs
1 level tablespoon clear honey
1 medium cooking apple,
  peeled, cored and grated

8 oz. self-raising flour
4 oz. sultanas
2 oz. chopped walnuts
Pinch of salt
1 level teaspoon mixed spice
Icing sugar to decorate

76

Pre-heat oven to 325°F/160°C/Gas Mark 3.

Combine the margarine and sugar. Add the eggs and a little flour and beat well. Beat in the honey and apple.

Add the sultanas, walnuts, salt and spice to the flour, mix and then fold into the honey mixture.

Turn into a greased and lined loaf tin about 8½ in. × 4½ in. × 2½ in. deep, and bake in the centre of the oven for about 1 hour, until cooked.

Turn out and cool on wire rack and, when cold, dredge with icing sugar.

Can be served sliced with butter.

BANANA AND WALNUT TEA-BREAD

Makes two small loaves

6 oz. margarine	2 ripe bananas
6 oz. sugar	2 oz. chopped walnuts
1 tablespoon hot water	8 oz. plain wholemeal flour
3 eggs	1 teaspoon baking powder

Pre-heat oven to 400°F/200°C/Gas Mark 6.

Oil two 1 lb. loaf tins, line with oiled greaseproof paper.

Beat margarine, sugar and hot water until light and fluffy.

Add the eggs, bananas and walnuts and beat until well mixed.

Fold in flour and baking powder.

Divide mixture into the two tins and bake for 20 minutes at 400°F/200°C/Gas Mark 6, and then for a further 20 minutes at 225°F/110°C/Gas Mark ¼.

Remove from oven and place upside-down on rack. Allow to cool before removing from tins.

CARROT AND COCONUT BREAD

Makes one 1 lb. loaf

3 eggs	1 cup chopped walnuts (and/or other nuts)
½ cup salad oil	
1 teaspoon vanilla flavouring	1 cup raisins
2 cups desiccated coconut	2 cups finely shredded carrot

2 cups plain flour
½ teaspoon salt
1 teaspoon baking powder
1 teaspoon bicarbonate of soda
1 teaspoon cinnamon
¾ cup sugar

Pre-heat oven to 350°F/180°C/Gas Mark 4.
Beat the eggs in a very large bowl until light in colour. Stir in salad oil,
    vanilla, coconut and nuts. Mix well.
Mix together the remaining ingredients, sifting all except the sugar, and
    stir into the first mixture. When well blended, spoon into a buttered
    and floured 1 lb. loaf tin (7½ in. × 4 in.) and bake for about 1 hour,
    until skewer comes out clean.
Remove from tin, wrap in tea towel and stand on rack to cool.

Can be kept wrapped in foil in fridge for weeks – its flavour will actually
    improve.

CHEESE SCONES

Makes approx. 16

8 oz. self-raising flour
Pinch salt
1 level teaspoon baking powder
1½ oz. butter (or margarine)
3–4 oz. Cheddar cheese, finely grated
1 level teaspoon mustard powder
1 dessertspoon tarragon
    vinegar made up to ¼ pint
    with milk

Pre-heat oven to 425°F/220°C/Gas Mark 7.
Grease baking sheet.
Sift flour, salt and baking powder into bowl, rub in butter.
Stir in half the cheese, the mustard and sufficient vinegar/milk to give
    fairly soft, light dough.
Roll out on lightly floured surface to about ¾ in. thick. Cut into rounds
    with 2 in. plain cutter. Put on baking sheet, brush tops with milk and
    sprinkle with the remaining cheese.
Bake in oven for about 10 minutes.
Cool on a wire rack.

DATE LOAF

Makes one 1 lb. loaf

½ lb. chopped dates
1 cup boiling water
Salt
½ teaspoon bicarbonate of soda

1 tablespoon butter
½ cup sugar
1 egg, beaten
1¼ cups self-raising flour

Grease a 1 lb. loaf tin.
Soak dates in water and add pinch of salt and bicarbonate of soda.
Beat butter and sugar and add egg. Add flour and date mixture
   alternately, mixing well.
Bake in loaf tin at 350°F/180°C/Gas Mark 4 for 30–45 minutes.

GRIDDLE SCONES

Makes 8–10

8 oz. self-raising flour
Pinch of salt
½ level teaspoon freshly grated
   nutmeg

2 oz. butter (or hard margarine)
2 oz. caster sugar
1 egg, beaten
3–4 tablespoons of milk

Pre-heat and grease griddle or heavy-bottomed frying pan.
Sift flour, salt and nutmeg together. Rub in fat. Stir in sugar. Mix in egg
   and milk to make a firm dough.
On a lightly floured surface, roll out to ½ in. thick. Cut into rounds or
   triangles. Cook on moderately hot griddle until brown on both sides
   – about 10 minutes.

Variation: Add 2 oz. dried fruit with the sugar.

IRISH BRACK

Makes one 1 lb. loaf

1 cup brown sugar dissolved in
   1 cup strong black coffee
1 lb. dried mixed fruit

2 cups self-raising flour
1 large (or 2 small) eggs, well
   beaten

Soak the dried fruit in the coffee/sugar mixture overnight.
Add the flour and the egg and mix well. Pour into well-greased 1 lb. loaf
tin, and bake for 2 hours at 300°F/150°C/Gas Mark 2.
Do not cut until the following day.

Slice thinly and spread with butter.

OVEN SCONES

Makes 10–12

8 oz. self-raising flour
½ level teaspoon salt
1 level teaspoon baking powder
1–2 oz. butter (or margarine)
¼ pint milk
Beaten egg or milk to glaze

Pre-heat oven to 450°F/230°C/Gas Mark 8.
Sift flour, salt and baking powder into a bowl. Rub in fat until mixture
resembles fine breadcrumbs. Make a well in the centre and stir in
enough milk to give a fairly soft dough.
Turn out on to lightly floured surface and knead very gently if necessary
to remove any cracks. Roll out to about ¾ in. thick. Cut into 10 to 12
rounds with a 2 in. cutter. Place on greased backing sheet, brush with
beaten egg or milk.
Bake towards the top of the oven for 8–10 minutes, until brown and well
risen. Turn on to wire rack to cool.

Serve split and buttered.

Variations:
EVERYDAY FRUIT SCONES Add 2 oz. currants, sultanas or chopped
dates (or a mixture of fruit) to the basic dry mixture.

RICH AFTERNOON TEA SCONES Follow basic recipe adding 1–2
level teaspoons caster sugar to dry ingredients and using 1 beaten
egg with 5 tablespoons of water or milk in place of ¼ pint of milk. 2
oz. dried fruit may also be added.

POTATO BREAD

Makes one 1 lb. loaf

8 oz. strong plain flour
2 level teaspoons baking
    powder
1 level teaspoon salt
6 oz. potatoes, cooked and
    mashed
1 tablespoon vegetable oil
Paprika for dusting

Pre-heat oven to 450°F/230°C/Gas Mark 8.
Grease a 1 lb. loaf tin, and line the base.
Mix together flour, baking powder and salt in bowl. Rub in mashed
    potato until evenly mixed with other ingredients.
Stir in oil and 7 fl. oz. water to make quite a wet dough.
Turn into the prepared loaf tin and dust surface with paprika.
Bake for about 25 minutes.
Turn out and cool on a wire rack.

SODA BREAD (1)

Serves 4

1 lb. plain flour
1 level teaspoon salt
1 level teaspoon bicarbonate of
    soda
12 fl. oz. buttermilk (or sour milk, or milk with 1 dessertspoon white
    vinegar stirred into it)

Pre-heat oven to 425°F/220°C/Gas Mark 7.
Sift dry ingredients into a bowl, and stir in the buttermilk to make a soft
    dough.
Turn on to well-floured board and knead lightly until smooth.
Shape into an 8 in. round and place on a greased baking sheet. Mark
    bread into quarters (called 'farls') and bake for 25–30 minutes, until
    golden-brown.

Serve split and buttered.

CAKES

AMIRA'S JIFFY CAKE

1 egg
½ cup cocoa
1 cup sugar
1½ cups plain flour, sifted
½ cup oil (or melted fat)
½ cup sour milk

1 teaspoon bicarbonate of soda
½ cup hot water
1 teaspoon vanilla essence
   (optional)
½ teaspoon salt

Pre-heat oven to 350°F/180°C/Gas Mark 4.
Put all ingredients in bowl in above order. Mix and beat until blended.
   It should be a runny consistency.
Put mixture in a greased and lined 7 in. baking tin. Bake for 30 minutes
   or until cooked. Allow to cool slightly in tin then turn out on to wire
   rack.
Cut in half, fill and cover in butter icing (see recipe on page 98) flavoured
   with chocolate, mocha, coffee or lemon.

APPLE COURTING CAKE

1 lb. cooking apples, stewed
   and sweetened, and beaten
   until fluffy, using little or no
   water to cook them
Short Pastry:
   8 oz. self-raising flour
   4 oz. lard
Sponge cake:
   2 oz. sugar
   2 oz. margarine
   4 oz. self-raising flour
   1 egg
   A little water

Butter icing:
   3 oz. icing sugar
   3 oz. butter (or margarine)

Pre-heat oven to 425°F/220°C/Gas Mark 7.

Make the pastry (for method see page 9).

Line a greased tin, approx. 10 in. × 7 in., with pastry. Allow apple to cool and spread over pastry.

Make sponge mixture by beating sugar and margarine to a cream and adding flour and beaten egg alternately with a little water until a thick and creamy mixture results. Spread over apple and cook in middle of oven for 25 minutes.

When cool spread with butter icing made by beating butter (or margarine) and icing sugar together. Furrow with a fork to decorate.

APPLE HARVEST CAKE

1¼ cups plain flour
1 cup wholewheat flour
1 cup white sugar
¾ cup soft brown sugar
1 level tablespoon cinnamon
2 teaspoons baking powder
1 level teaspoon salt
½ teaspoon bicarbonate of soda

¾ cup vegetable or corn oil
1 teaspoon vanilla flavouring
3 large eggs
2 cups peeled and finely chopped apples
½ cup chopped nuts or sultanas

Pre-heat oven to 325°F/160°C/Gas Mark 3.

Mix all ingredients (except the apples and nuts or sultanas) in a large bowl. Fold in the apples and nuts once other ingredients are thoroughly mixed.

Bake in a large greased ring baking tin, or two large layer cake tins, for about 45–50 minutes, until done.

N.B. Use a full teacup if you do not own a US 8 oz. measuring cup.

APPLE, SULTANA AND CINNAMON CAKE

¼ pint apple juice
4 oz. soft brown sugar
4 oz. sultanas
4 oz. butter
8 oz. Bramley or eating apples, peeled, cored and chopped

2 eggs
10 oz. wholemeal self-raising flour
1 teaspoon ground cinnamon
1 oz. demerara sugar

Pre-heat oven to 350°F/180°C/Gas Mark 4.

Place apple juice, sugar, sultanas and butter in large saucepan. Heat until butter melts and then simmer for 5 minutes. Allow mixture to cool.

Add apples and beaten eggs and mix well. Fold in flour and cinnamon.

Place mixture into a prepared 7 in. tin and sprinkle top with demerara sugar. Bake for 60–75 minutes, until cake is golden brown and firm to touch.

Stand for 5 minutes and then turn out on to wire rack to cool.

BLACKBERRY CAKE

4 oz. butter
4 oz. sugar
1 egg
8 oz. plain flour
2 teaspoons baking powder
¼ teaspoon salt
¼ pint milk

Topping:
8 oz. ripe blackberries
2 oz. butter
4 oz. sugar
2 oz. flour
½ teaspoon cinnamon

Pre-heat oven to 350°F/180°C/Gas Mark 4.

Cream butter and sugar and beat in the egg. Gradually add flour sifted with baking powder and salt, and beat to a smooth batter with the milk. Pour into greased rectangular tin (about 7 in. × 11 in.). Sprinkle thickly with washed and drained blackberries (reserving a few for top).

Make topping: Cream butter and sugar and work in the flour and cinnamon to a crumbled consistency. Sprinkle over blackberries and decorate with a few blackberries on top. Bake for 1 hour.

Cool in tin.

BOTER KOEK (BUTTER CAKE)

8 oz. butter (or half butter, half margarine)
8 oz. soft brown sugar
1 level teaspoon finely grated lemon rind

1 standard egg
8 oz. plain flour
2 oz. chopped crystallized ginger or chopped almonds (optional)

Pre-heat oven to 350°F/180°C/Gas Mark 4.

Cream butter and sugar and add lemon rind. Beat in egg and gently fold in flour and ginger or almonds. Spread in prepared Swiss roll tin, approx. 8 in. × 12 in.

Bake in centre of oven for 45–50 minutes or until golden. Cool slightly and cut into squares or fingers – about 24 pieces.

Store in airtight tin when cold.

CANADIAN BUTTER TARTS

8 oz. shortcrust pastry

Butter Tart filling:

2 tablespoons butter	1 egg, beaten
6 oz. soft brown sugar	½ teaspoon vanilla
⅛ teaspoon salt	flavouring
	5½ oz. currants

Pre-heat oven to 400°F/200°C/Gas Mark 6.

Make shortcrust pastry (for method see page 9).

Line greased patty tins with shortcrust pastry.

Melt butter in a saucepan and add the sugar. Remove from heat and cool for 5 minutes then add salt, beaten egg, vanilla and currants. Drop teaspoonfuls of the mixture into lined patty tins and bake for approx. 15–20 minutes.

N.B. This filling will bubble over if patty tins are too full.

CARROT CAKE

2 eggs	1½ teaspoons cinnamon
1 cup raw sugar	½ teaspoon ginger
¾ cup vegetable oil	1 teaspoon nutmeg
1 cup wholemeal self-raising flour	2½ cups grated carrot (about 8 oz.)
	¾ cup walnut pieces

Pre-heat oven to 350°F/180°C/Gas Mark 4.

Grease a 7 in. square tin at least 1½ in. deep.

Mix eggs, raw sugar and vegetable oil together. Add flour and spices and mix well. Add carrot and walnuts. Turn into tin and bake for 1 hour.

CARROT CAKE (PASSION CAKE)

6 fl. oz. corn oil
6 oz. caster sugar
3 eggs
1 teaspoon vanilla essence
1 teaspoon salt
8 oz. carrots, grated
6 oz. plain flour
1 teaspoon bicarbonate of soda
1 teaspoon baking powder
1 teaspoon cinnamon
4 oz. walnuts

Frosting:
  3 oz. Philadelphia (or low fat)
  cheese
  3 oz. butter (or sunflower
  margarine)
  ½ teaspoon almond essence
  4 oz. icing sugar
Walnut pieces to decorate

Pre-heat oven to 350°F/180°C/Gas Mark 4.

Place all cake ingredients (except walnuts) in a food processor and blend. Stir in the walnuts. Place in a prepared 8 in. cake tin and bake for approx. 1 hour 15 minutes.

When cooked, cake should spring from the sides of the tin. Cool in the tin.

For the frosting, beat all the ingredients together until creamy. 'Frost' the top of the cake and decorate with walnut pieces.

N.B. If the cake is mixed in the conventional way, grate the carrot.

CHARLTON CAKE

4 oz. butter (or margarine)
4 oz. caster sugar
2 oz. glacé cherries, chopped
3 oz. sultanas
2 dessertspoons golden syrup

6 oz. self-raising flour
2 oz. wholemeal flour, self-raising if possible
1 heaped teaspoon baking powder

Pre-heat oven to 375°F/190°C/Gas Mark 5.

Melt fat and sugar on low heat then mix in other ingredients. Spread mixture in prepared shallow square tin (approx. 8 in.) and bake for 20 minutes.

Cut into squares while warm.

CHERRY AND ALMOND CAKE

5 oz. margarine (or butter)
4 oz. caster sugar
2 eggs
3 oz. self-raising flour
2 oz. ground almonds
2 oz. glacé cherries, chopped
1 teaspoon almond essence

Pre-heat oven to 350°F/180°C/Gas Mark 4.
Cream together margarine and sugar until light and fluffy. Add beaten eggs and rest of ingredients and mix well. Turn into a greased and lined 2 lb. loaf tin.
Bake for 40 minutes. If not cooked after 40 minutes, place greaseproof paper over top of cake to prevent too much browning, reduce heat and leave until cooked.
Cool on a wire rack.

CHOCOLATE CAKE

A moist cake which keeps well

3 oz. drinking chocolate
3 oz. soft margarine
2 tablespoons golden syrup
2 tablespoons warm water
2 standard eggs, beaten
3 oz. self-raising flour

Pre-heat oven to 350°F/180°C/Gas Mark 4.
Place chocolate, margarine, syrup and water in a bowl and beat until mixture looks bubbly. Beat in eggs. Fold in flour.
Pour into prepared 6–6½ in. cake tin. Bake for 30 minutes in middle of oven until risen and firm to touch.
Cool slightly in tin before turning out.
Can be layered when cold. Decorate as liked.

CHRISTMAS CAKE

N.B. Soak fruit (Group 4) in half a cup of brandy for at least 24 hours, stirring often.

New Circo them 140° cook 4 cakes to-gether 8" takes 2 hr 30 min
6" " " 2 hrs appro

Group 1:
½ lb. brown sugar
1 oz. glycerine
1 oz. treacle
1 oz. malt
8 oz. margarine
Pinch nutmeg
Pinch spice

Group 2:
5 eggs
1 tablespoon milk
½ cup brandy
½ teaspoon lemon essence
½ teaspoon almond essence

Group 3:
8 oz. plain flour

Group 4:
3 lb. mixed fruit
6 oz. glacé cherries chopped
in 2 or 3 pieces
3 oz. flaked almonds (if
desired)

Group 5:
8 oz. plain flour
1 teaspoon baking powder

NB. Two mixtures
makes 4 cakes
don't try in 3 tins ie.
(8"+2 7"+1)+ 6½"×1

Pre-heat oven to 300°F/150°C/Gas Mark 2.

Thoroughly mix ingredients from Group 1. Beat till soft but do not cream. Add all liquid ingredients, Group 2, then add Group 3 immediately. Beat lightly for about 5 minutes then stir in ingredients from Group 4 and Group 5 and mix thoroughly.

Turn into greased and lined 8 in. cake tin and bake in oven for 2½ hours.

When cooked, sprinkle freely with brandy while cake is still hot. Then cover with greaseproof paper and cloth until cold.

Makes approximately 5 lb. cake when cooked.

10" petal tin allow + 15 mins
12" SQ - 1½ times mixture test after 3 hrs

COFFEE MERINGUE GATEAU*

Meringue:
4 egg whites
8 oz. caster sugar

Butter cream:
4 oz. granulated sugar
5 tablespoons water

4 egg yolks
12 oz. unsalted butter
1 dessertspoon coffee
dissolved in 2 teaspoons hot
water
4 oz. toasted flaked almonds

Pre-heat oven to 300°F/150°C/Gas Mark 2.

Make meringue by whisking egg whites until fairly stiff, add half the sugar. When beginning to stiffen, gradually add remaining sugar, continue whisking. Spread on to three baking sheets lined with non-stick paper marked out in 9 in. rings. Bake for 60–80 minutes.

To make butter cream dissolve sugar in water over low heat and bring to the boil for 2–3 minutes until 225°F is reached. Pour syrup on to egg yolks, whisking all the time until thick mousse is formed. Add soft beaten butter a little at a time and finally, coffee mixture. Pour on to meringue bases to cover. Coat with 4 oz. toasted flaked almonds.

This freezes very well but do not put the almond flakes on until thawed out.

CONTINENTAL GATEAU

(Very rich!)

3 oz. unbleached walnuts or
    almonds
½ pint milk
4 oz. butter
4 oz. icing sugar
4 egg yolks
1 lb. boudoir biscuits
¼ pint double cream
Rum

Grease a 7 in round tin with push-out base.

Grate or chop nuts finely. Boil scant ½ cup milk and pour over nuts.

Cream butter and sugar until fluffy. Stir in nut mixture and beat in egg yolks.

Pour rest of milk into shallow bowl and flavour with rum (do not use rum essence). Dip biscuits for few seconds. Line base of tin with the wet biscuits.

Spread thickly with creamed nut mixture and continue in alternate layers. Place flat plate (greased slightly) on top, then a heavy weight and leave for at least 2 hours in cool place (overnight is best).

Push out on to serving plate. Spread top with whipped cream and decorate.

CRUSTY LEMON BUTTER CAKE

6 oz. melted butter
6 oz. caster sugar
2 eggs
6 oz. self-raising flour
Topping:
    4 oz. caster sugar
    Juice of 1 lemon

Pre-heat oven to 350°F/180°C/Gas Mark 4.
Grease a 14 in. × 9 in. tin.
Melt butter and stir in sugar. Beat eggs and stir into mixture with flour.
    Pour into tin and bake for 35–40 minutes.
Remove from oven. Mix topping ingredients together and while cake is
    still hot, pour over in a thin layer. The juice sinks into the surface of
    the cake leaving the top crispy when it is cold.

CUT AND COME AGAIN CAKE

1 lb. self-raising flour
4 oz. caster sugar
4–8 oz. dried mixed fruit
3 dessertspoons golden syrup
1–2 eggs
Milk or milk and water to mix

Pre-heat oven to 350°F/180°C/Gas Mark 4.
Mix flour, sugar and dried fruit in a bowl. Add golden syrup, beaten
    eggs in milk, and mix well until it reaches the consistency of stiff,
    sticky dough.
Place in a greased 2 lb. loaf tin. Cook for 50–60 minutes.
When cool, turn out on to wire rack.

A very economical cake. Use whatever ingredients you have available
    (e.g. 1 or 2 eggs, milk or milk and water). When the cake is cooked
    and cold, slice thinly and spread with butter. It makes a very nice tea-
    time snack.

FESTIVE FRUIT CAKE

(Expensive but delicious!)

8 oz. dessert dates
8 oz. glacé pineapple
4 oz. glacé appricots
4 oz. red glacé cherries
4 oz. green glacé cherries
8 oz. brazil nuts
2 eggs
½ cup brown sugar

1 tablespoon rum
1 teaspoon vanilla essence
3 oz. butter
¼ cup plain flour
¼ cup self-raising flour
¼ teaspoon salt
1 tablespoon rum (for top of cake)

Pre-heat oven to 325°F/160°C/Gas Mark 3.

Grease a 9 in. × 5 in. loaf tin. Line with greased paper.

Stone and halve dates. Chop pineapple and apricots into large pieces. Leave cherries and nuts whole.

Beat eggs until thick and creamy, add sugar, rum and vanilla and beat until sugar is dissolved. Add softened butter and beat until combined. Stir in sifted flours and salt. Add fruit and nuts and mix thoroughly.

Spread evenly in tin and bake for 1½–2 hours. When cooked, remove from oven and brush with extra rum, cover with foil and leave until cold.

When cold, remove from tin and rewrap in foil until required.

FOOLPROOF SPONGE

2 eggs
4 oz. sugar
2 oz. butter or margarine

3 fl. oz. milk
4 oz. plain flour
2 teaspoons baking powder

Pre-heat oven to 325°F/160°C/Gas Mark 3.

Beat eggs and sugar to thick cream. Melt the butter in the milk. Sift flour and baking powder. Add to the egg mixture. Add the melted butter and milk.

Pour into two greased and lined 7 in. sandwich tins and bake for 15–20 minutes.

This versatile recipe can be used with cocoa to make chocolate cake; with cherries and dried fruit; or cooked in a bread tin to use as hot sponge pudding with syrup.

FRUIT CAKE

(Suitable for children to make)

1 oz. glacé cherries
4 oz. currants
4 oz. raisins
2 oz. mixed peel
5 oz. margarine
¼ pint water
6 oz. tin sweetened condensed
   milk
5 oz. plain flour
½ level teaspoon bicarbonate of
   soda
Pinch salt

Pre-heat oven to 335°F/170°C/Gas Mark 3 ½.
Heat cherries, currants, raisins, mixed peel, margarine and water in a
   saucepan and simmer for 3 minutes. Allow to cool. Add condensed
   milk, flour, bicarbonate of soda and salt and stir well.
Put mixture in greased and lined 7 in. cake tin and cook for 1¼ hours.

LAVINIA'S DORSET APPLE CAKE

8 oz. self-raising flour
4 oz. margarine
Pinch salt
4 oz. sugar
2 oz. currants
12 oz. apples, chopped
Milk

Topping:
2–3 oz. butter
1 heaped tablespoon
   demerara sugar
Pinch cinnamon

Pre-heat oven to 350°F/180°C/Gas Mark 4.
Rub in flour, margarine, salt and sugar. Add currants and chopped
   apples. Add milk to mix to a dropping consistency.
Put in 7 in. or 8 in. greased baking tin and cook for about 1 hour.
Whilst cake is still warm, mix topping ingredients together (except
   cinnamon) and spread over top so it partly melts into cake. Sprinkle
   cinnamon on top.

MILK CHOCOLATE CAKE

7 oz. self-raising flour
8 oz. caster sugar
¾ teaspoon salt
2 tablespoons cocoa
4 oz. margarine

2 eggs
5 tablespoons evaporated milk
5 tablespoons water
1 teaspoon vanilla essence

Pre-heat oven to 325°-350°F/160°-180°C/Gas Mark 3–4.
Sift together flour, sugar, salt and cocoa. Rub in margarine. Beat eggs
    with evaporated milk, water and vanilla essence. Stir into flour
    mixture and beat well.
Grease and flour two deep 7 in. cake tins (not loose-bottomed as the
    mixture will run out).
Bake for about 35 minutes.
When cold, sandwich together with either plain or chocolate butter icing
    (see page 98) and cover with milk chocolate icing (see page 109).

An equal quantity of carob powder can be substituted for cocoa – it is
    less bitter and, as it is sweeter, the sugar can be reduced by 1 oz.

MOIST EVERYDAY FRUIT CAKE

4 oz. butter or margarine
4 oz. light brown sugar
2 eggs (size 3)
6 oz. self-raising flour

Pinch salt
2 oz. ground almonds
2 dessertspoons marmalade
6 oz. sultanas

Pre-heat oven to 325°F/160°C/Gas Mark 3.
Prepare 6 in. baking tin.
Cream fat and sugar. Add beaten eggs. Sift dry ingredients together and
    fold in. Finally stir in fruit and marmalade.
Bake in lower part of oven for 1¾ hours.

NESSIE'S CHOCOLATE CAKE

2 oz. butter
4 oz. caster sugar
3 eggs

4 oz. drinking chocolate
2 oz. self-raising flour
2 oz. ground almonds

Pre-heat oven to 325°F/160°C/Gas Mark 3.

Cream together butter and caster sugar and gradually work in eggs. Mix together the drinking chocolate, flour and ground almonds and fold into the mixture.

Grease and line a small deep tin (not a large flat one) either 6 in. round or 5 in. square. Pour in the mixture.

Cook for 1 hour.

This cake improves with keeping.

PINEAPPLE CAKE

4 oz. margarine
6 oz. soft brown sugar
12 oz. mixed fruit
7 oz. tin crushed pineapple

4 oz. glacé cherries
8 oz. self-raising flour
2 eggs

Pre-heat oven to 350°F/180°C/Gas Mark 4.

Put all ingredients, except flour and eggs, into saucepan. Bring to boil stirring all the time. Cool slightly then beat in eggs one at a time. Fold in flour.

Turn mixture into prepared 2 lb. loaf tin and bake for 1 ¾ hours.

THE QUEEN MOTHER'S CAKE

4 oz. dates, stoned and
  chopped
1 teaspoon bicarbonate of soda
6 oz. sugar
2 oz. butter
6 oz. plain flour
2 oz. walnuts, chopped
1 egg
1 teaspoon vanilla essence
½ teaspoon salt
1 teaspoon baking powder

Topping:
  3 tablespoons soft light
  brown sugar
  1 tablespoon butter
  1 tablespoon top of milk or
  single cream
Chopped nuts

Pre-heat oven to 350°F/180°C/Gas Mark 4.

Line a Swiss roll tin with foil.

Pour 1 cup boiling water over the dates. Add the bicarbonate of soda. Leave to stand.

Meanwhile mix together sugar, butter, flour, walnuts, egg, vanilla essence, salt and baking powder. Add to the date mixture. Place mixture in tin and bake for 35 minutes.

To make topping, mix all ingredients together and bring to the boil for 3 minutes. Spread on top of the cake and decorate with chopped nuts. Cut into squares or fingers.

This cake is said to be the Queen Mother's favourite!

SHIRLEY'S HERMITS

4½ oz. butter	¼ teaspoon ground nutmeg
3 oz. caster sugar	¼ teaspoon ground mace
2 eggs	¼ teaspoon ground cloves
4 fl. oz. black treacle	¼ teaspoon allspice
4 oz. plain flour	2 oz. chopped walnuts
1½ teaspoons baking powder	8 oz. raisins
1 teaspoon ground cinnamon	

Pre-heat oven to 350°F/180°C/Gas Mark 4.

Beat together the butter, caster sugar and eggs. Add black treacle and beat. Stir in sifted dry ingredients, together with chopped walnuts and raisins.

Spread on greased, lined Swiss roll tin, and bake for 15–20 minutes.

Cool in tin. Cut into squares or fingers.

Ice if desired with lemon icing made with 1 tablespoon lemon juice and 4 oz. icing sugar.

SPICED SANDWICH

4 oz. butter	1 teaspoon baking powder
4 oz. sugar	2 teaspoons ground ginger
2 eggs	1 teaspoon ground nutmeg
½ cup golden syrup	½ cup milk
4 oz. plain flour	½ teaspoon bicarbonate of soda

95

Icing:
  3 tablespoons butter
  6 tablespoons icing sugar
  Few drops vanilla essence (to
  taste)
Desiccated coconut

Pre-heat oven to 350°F/180°C/Gas Mark 4.

Cream butter and sugar. Add eggs one at a time and beat well. Using a wooden spoon add golden syrup, then sifted flour, baking powder, ginger and nutmeg. Dissolve bicarbonate of soda in the milk and add to the cake mixture.

Turn into two prepared 7 in. sandwich tins. Bake for 40–45 minutes. When cooked, turn on to wire rack to cool.

Make up icing by creaming together all the icing ingredients. Put half the icing on each cake and sandwich together. Sprinkle the top with some desiccated coconut.

This cake can also be cooked in one square tin (9in. or 10 in.). This is a good idea if the cake is for cutting up at functions. This is an Australian recipe and therefore the cup measurement used is approximately the equivalent of a breakfast cup. The mixture is very wet.

SWISS APPLE CAKE

4 oz. butter
2 oz. sugar
1 egg
8 oz. plain flour
2 teaspoons baking powder

Few drops vanilla essence
1 lb. cooked apple or other
  suitable drained fruit
Jam

Pre-heat oven to 350°F/180°C/Gas Mark 4.

Cream butter and sugar, add egg, sifted flour, baking powder and vanilla essence, mix well.

Place half the dough on a large 10 in. greased Pyrex plate, spread evenly. Spread with jam and then add cooked fruit. Take marble-sized pieces from other half of dough and place on top of fruit until roughly covered. Edge plate with a little of the dough mixture as it gives a more finished look.

Bake for approximately 45 minutes until golden brown.

Dust with icing sugar and serve with cream or custard.

VICTORIAN CHRISTMAS CAKE

1 lb. mixed fruit
4 oz. stoned and chopped
    raisins
4 oz. glacé cherries
¼ pint sweet sherry
6 oz. soft margarine
6 oz. moist brown sugar
Grated rind of 1 lemon

Grated rind of 1 orange
3 eggs
1 tablespoon black treacle
2 oz. chopped blanched
    almonds
4 oz. plain flour
2 oz. self-raising flour
1 teaspoon mixed spice

Soak fruit in sherry for 3 days.
Pre-heat oven to 275°F/130°C/Gas Mark 1.
Beat margarine and sugar together. Add all ingredients to soaked fruit.
    Mix well.
Place in prepared 7 in. cake tin and bake in the centre of oven for 3½
    hours.

WHOLEMEAL SPONGE

(Plain or Chocolate)

4 oz. margarine
4 oz. caster sugar
4 oz. wholemeal plain flour
1 teaspoon baking powder
2 eggs

2 oz. drinking chocolate (if
    required)

Pre-heat oven to 400°F/200°C/Gas Mark 6.
Put margarine and sugar in bowl and beat well until fluffy and pale.
    Add dessertspoon of flour and 1 egg and mix. Repeat and mix for 3
    minutes or until thoroughly mixed to creamy consistency.
Fold in flour and baking powder (and chocolate if required) in small
    quantities with metal spoon until the mixture falls off spoon. If it does
    not, add a little milk.
Oil two 6 in. sandwich tins with cooking oil, line with greaseproof
    paper, and oil paper. Divide mixture between the tins.
Cook for 30 minutes or until the sponge springs back if gently pressed.
    Remove from oven, place upside down on cooling rack.
Allow to cool before removing tins.
Sandwich together and top with butter icing (see recipe on page 98).

BISCUITS

ALMOND MACAROONS

Makes 18

2 egg whites (size 2)
4 oz. ground almonds
8 oz. caster sugar
½ oz. ground rice

½ teaspoon vanilla essence
½ teaspoon almond essence
A little extra egg white
9 blanched and split almonds

Pre-heat oven to 325°F/160°C/Gas Mark 3.

Brush one or two baking trays with melted butter and line with rice paper.

Beat egg whites until foamy but not stiff. Add ground almonds, sugar, ground rice and vanilla and almond essence and beat well.

Pipe or spoon 18 mounds of mixture, well spaced, on to prepared tray or trays. Brush with egg white. Put half an almond in the middle of each mound.

Bake in centre of oven for 20–25 minutes or until pale gold. Leave on trays for 5 minutes.

Carefully lift off and remove rice paper from around the edges of each. Cool on wire rack. Store in airtight tin when cold.

AUSTRALIAN SHORTBREAD BUTTONS

Makes approx. 24–30

6 oz. soft margarine
2 oz. icing sugar
6 oz. plain flour

2 oz. custard powder
Few drops vanilla essence

Pre-heat oven to 370°F/185°C/Gas Mark 4 ½.

Cream margarine and icing sugar. Add flour and custard powder and mix thoroughly. Add vanilla essence and mix.

Take teaspoons of mixture and roll into balls. Place on greased baking tray and press flat with a wet fork.

Bake for approx. 15 minutes.

CHOCOLATE CRISPS*

6 oz. butter (or margarine)
3 oz. caster sugar
5 oz. plain flour

2 oz. cornflakes, crushed
2 tablespoons cocoa powder
Few drops vanilla essence

Pre-heat oven to 350°F/180°C/Gas Mark 4.

Lightly grease a baking sheet.

Cream together the butter and sugar until light and fluffy. Stir in the flour, cornflakes, cocoa powder and vanilla essence. Mix together well until all the ingredients are thoroughly combined.

Drop small teaspoonfuls of the mixture on to the greased baking sheet and bake for approx. 20 minutes.

Allow the chocolate crisps to cool a little before lifting carefully on to a wire rack and leave until cooled.

These chocolate crisps freeze well.

DOROTHY'S CHERRY BARS

Makes approx. 15–20 bars

Base:
6 oz. plain flour
4 oz. margarine
2 tablespoons icing sugar

Topping:
9 oz. brown sugar
2 eggs, well beaten
4 oz. chopped walnuts
8 oz. glacé cherries, halved
½ teaspoon almond extract
2 teaspoons plain flour

Pre-heat oven to 350°F/180°C/Gas Mark 4.

To make base, rub margarine into flour until mixture resembles breadcrumbs. Add icing sugar. Press into a prepared 9 × 9 in. cake pan (or 7 × 11 in. or 9 × 13 in. pan) and bake for 10 minutes.

Whilst base is cooking, combine all the topping ingredients. Spread the topping over the partially cooked base and return to oven for a further 25–30 minutes.

Cut into bars.

If desired, ice the bars with a thin butter cream icing flavoured with Kirsch.

EASTER BISCUITS

Makes 24 biscuits

6 oz. margarine
4 oz. caster sugar
1 egg
2 ½–3 drops cassia

8 oz. plain flour
Pinch salt
2 oz. currants

Pre-heat oven to 350°F/180°C/Gas Mark 4.

Cream margarine and sugar until fluffy. Beat in the egg and cassia. Stir in the sieved flour, salt and currants.

Knead lightly to a smooth dough, chill in fridge for 1 hour if mixture is very soft.

Roll out thinly on floured surface, cut into rounds with 3 ¼ in. cutter. Put on lightly greased baking sheets and bake for about 12–15 minutes until lightly coloured.

Place on a wire rack to cool and dust with caster sugar.

Cassia is from a tree similar to cinnamon and gives a delicate flavour. It can be obtained from a chemist.

EVERSHOT CHOCY TREATS

Makes 18

4 oz. luxury margarine (from a
    tub)
2 oz. caster sugar
2 oz. brown sugar
¼ teaspoon salt
1 teaspoon vanilla essence
1 egg, beaten
4 oz. self-raising flour
1 ½ oz. rolled oats

Topping:
    2 oz. plain chocolate
    2 oz. chopped almonds

Pre-heat oven to 350°F/180°C/Gas Mark 4.

Beat fat, sugar, salt, vanilla and egg until pale and fluffy. Stir in flour and oats.

Spread in greased 9 in. square baking tin. Bake in centre of oven for 30 minutes. Remove from oven and leave in tin to cool.

To make topping, melt chocolate, pour over cooled cake and sprinkle with nuts. Cut cake into bars when cold.

FLORENTINES

Makes 12

3 oz. butter
4 tablespoons milk
4 oz. sifted icing sugar
2 oz. plain flour (do *not* use self-
   raising flour)

3 oz. chopped peel
2 oz. chopped glacé cherries
3 oz. flaked almonds
1 teaspoon lemon juice
4 oz. chocolate

Pre-heat oven to 375°F/190°C/Gas Mark 5.

Line flat tins with rice paper.

Put the butter, milk and icing sugar into a saucepan and heat until the
   butter is melted. Remove from the heat. Stir in the flour, peel,
   cherries, almonds and lemon juice. Leave until cold.

Spoon equal amounts of the mixture on to rice paper, well spaced to
   allow for spreading. Bake just above the centre of the oven for 10
   minutes, or until pale gold. Remove from oven and leave until
   lukewarm.

Carefully lift off the trays and trim off excess rice paper. Cool completely
   on a wire rack.

Melt chocolate in a basin over hot water. Spoon melted chocolate on to
   the rice paper side of each florentine and spread evenly with a knife.
   Mark wavy lines on each with a fork and leave until the chocolate
   hardens.

Store in an airtight tin.

LINCOLN CRISPS

Makes 15–20

5 oz. chopped salted peanuts
1 cup desiccated coconut
4 cups cornflakes, lightly
   crushed
2 egg whites
1 cup sugar
1 teaspoon vanilla essence
2 tablespoons melted butter

Pre-heat oven to 350°F/180°C/Gas Mark 4.

Place peanuts, coconut and cornflakes in a bowl and mix together. Whisk egg whites to a stiff froth and gradually beat in sugar and vanilla. Add dry mixture and melted butter and mix well. Place in small heaps on a well greased baking tray. Bake for 10 minutes or until lightly browned. Remove from tray when firm but not cold.

MOM'S CHRISTMAS SPICE COOKIES

Makes 20–24

4 oz. softened butter
4 oz. soft brown sugar
6 oz. plain flour
½ teaspoon ground cinnamon
¼ teaspoon each of ground
  cloves, nutmeg and allspice
1 large egg
6 oz. raisins

4 oz. walnuts, roughly chopped
5 oz. dates, chopped
6 oz. combination of glacé
  cherries and mixed glacé
  fruits such as melon,
  pineapple, etc.
½ teaspoon bicarbonate of soda
  mixed in 1½ fl. oz. hot water

Pre-heat oven to 375°F/190°C/Gas Mark 5.
Beat together butter and sugar. Mix together flour and spices. Add egg, followed by flour and mixed fruits alternately. Finally, mix in soda/water combination and blend well.
Drop teaspoonfuls on to greased baking sheet and bake for 8–10 minutes. Leave on baking sheet for a few minutes to 'set' before transferring them to a wire rack to cool.

NUTTY CRISPS

Makes 24

6 oz. margarine
2 oz. butter
3 oz. caster sugar
2 tablespoons hot water

2 scant teaspoons vanilla
  essence
8 oz. plain flour
2 oz. walnuts, chopped

Cream butter and margarine then add sugar, hot water, vanilla essence, flour and walnuts. Wrap dough in foil and leave in refrigerator at least 2 hours.
Pre-heat oven to 350°F/180°C/Gas Mark 4.
Roll dough into pencil shapes, cut into 3 in. lengths and curve into little crescents. Put on an *ungreased* baking sheet and bake for 15 minutes. Leave on baking sheet to cool.

ORANGE AND CHOCOLATE COOKIES

Makes 20–24

4 oz. margarine
3 oz. sugar
1 oz. golden syrup
6 oz. self-raising flour
Rind of one orange, finely
   grated
2–3 oz. chopped chocolate

Pre-heat oven to 325°F/160°C/Gas Mark 3.
Put margarine, sugar and syrup into a saucepan and heat gently until
   margarine melts, stirring occasionally. Mix flour with orange rind in a
   large bowl, make a well in the centre and pour the syrup into the
   centre and mix well.
Allow to become quite cold and then stir in the chopped chocolate.
Drop teaspoonfuls of the mixture on to greased baking trays, leaving a
   space between cookies to allow for spreading. Bake for 15 minutes.
Leave cookies to cool slightly before placing on wire racks to cool
   completely.

ORIGINAL CHOCOLATE CHIP COOKIES

Makes 24

1½ oz. granulated sugar
3 oz. soft brown sugar
4 oz. margarine
1 teaspoon vanilla essence
1 egg, beaten
6 oz. plain flour
½ teaspoon salt

½ teaspoon bicarbonate of soda
4 oz. chocolate chips

Pre-heat oven to 375°F/190°C/Gas Mark 5.
Beat together sugars, margarine and vanilla. Add beaten egg. Mix
   together flour, salt and bicarbonate of soda and then add to sugar
   mix. Finally, stir in chocolate chips.
Drop teaspoonfuls on to greased baking sheet and bake for 10 minutes.

PEANUT COOKIES

Makes 24

4 oz. salted peanuts
3 oz. soft margarine
3 oz. sugar
1 egg
5 oz. self-raising flour

Pre-heat oven to 350°F/180°C/Gas Mark 4.
Chop peanuts, reserving about 1 oz. for decoration. Cream margarine
and sugar, add egg and a little of the flour. Add nuts and remaining
flour alternately. Work in with a wooden spoon. It will be a stiff
mixture.
Spoon into little heaps on greased baking sheet and decorate with
remaining peanuts. Bake for 15 minutes. Leave on the baking tray for
a few minutes to 'set', transfer to a wire rack to cool.

QUEENSLAND FRUIT AND NUT COOKIES

Makes 20–24

4 oz. margarine
4 oz. peanut butter
Rind of one orange, grated
4 oz. caster sugar
1 egg
3 oz. sultanas, chopped
4 oz. plain flour
1½ teaspoons baking powder

Pre-heat oven to 350°F/180°C/Gas Mark 4.
Cream margarine, peanut butter, orange rind and sugar until light and
fluffy. Beat in egg, add sultanas. Mix together flour and baking
powder and add to mixture. Mix well.
Roll into balls the size of walnuts and place on greased baking sheet.
Criss-cross with a fork prior to baking for 12–15 minutes. Leave on
the baking tray for a few minutes to 'set', transfer to a wire rack to
cool.

TEA-TIME TOFFEE BARS

Makes 18

4 oz. butter (or margarine)
4 oz. soft brown sugar
1 egg yolk
2 oz. plain flour
2 oz. porridge oats

Topping:
8 oz. plain chocolate
1 oz. butter
Chopped walnuts

Pre-heat oven to 375°F/190°C/Gas Mark 5.
Grease a Swiss roll tin.
Beat butter, sugar and egg yolk. Add flour and oats and mix.
Press mixture into tin and bake for 15–20 minutes. Cool slightly.
For topping, melt butter and chocolate and spread over the mixture and
   cover with chopped walnuts. Cut into bars while warm but leave in
   tin until cold.

WHOLEMEAL NUT BISCUITS

Makes 40

8 oz. wholemeal plain flour
10 oz. porridge oats
8 oz. hard margarine
2 level teaspoons bicarbonate of
   soda
3 drops vanilla essence
3 oz. bran
6 oz. brown sugar
6 oz. caster sugar
2 eggs (size 3)
2 oz. chopped nuts

Pre-heat oven to 300°F/150°C/Gas Mark 2.
Put all ingredients into bowl and mix to stiff paste. (Add more flour if
   too wet.)
Spread kitchen foil on baking tray and oil with vegetable oil.
Flour hands and roll mixture into 'walnut' sized balls.
Place balls on tray, leaving them room to spread. Bake for 10–15 minutes
   or until brown.
Place biscuits on wire rack and allow to cool.

SPECIAL DIET – GLUTEN FREE

BUTTER SQUARES

Makes 12

4 oz. butter
2 oz. brown sugar
2 oz. caster sugar
2 teaspoons cinnamon
2 teaspoons mixed spice

1 egg yolk
6 oz. gluten free plain flour
1 teaspoon gluten free baking
   powder
Chopped almonds for top

Pre-heat oven to 350°F/180°C/Gas Mark 4.
Cream butter and sugar then add spices and egg yolk. Sift in flour and
   baking powder and mix well. Press mixture into greased 11 in. × 7 in.
   tin. Sprinkle nuts on top and press lightly.
Bake for 20–25 minutes. Cut into squares while hot and leave to cool
   before removing from the tin.

GROUND RICE CURRANT CAKE

4 oz. margarine
4 oz. caster sugar
2 eggs
6 oz. ground rice
3 oz. currants

1 teaspoon gluten free baking
   powder
Pinch salt
Milk to mix

Pre-heat oven to 350°F/180°C/Gas Mark 4.
Cream margarine and sugar. Beat in the eggs. Stir in the dry
ingredients. Add 2–3 tablespoons milk to make a soft consistency.
Turn mixture into prepared 6 in. baking tin. Bake for about 50 minutes.
Leave in tin for a few minutes then turn out carefully on to a wire rack.

GROUND RICE PUDDING

3 rounded dessertspoons
   ground rice
1 pint made up coconut milk powder

Knob of margarine (or butter)
Sweetener of your choice

Mix ground rice with enough coconut milk to make a paste. Boil rest of
   coconut milk, add rice paste and continue to simmer until thick,
   about 3 minutes. Add small knob of margarine (or butter) and
   sweeten to taste.
Serve hot, or set in mould and serve as a cold sweet with fruit if liked.

This is an ideal recipe for those allergic to dairy products. Coconut milk
   powder can also be used for hot drinks, e.g. cocoa, Ovaltine.

NUT BROWNIES

Makes 10

1 egg white
2½ oz. brown sugar
2½ oz. ground nuts (almonds,
walnuts, hazel nuts, or mixed nuts)

1 level tablespoon ground rice
Rind of half an orange, grated

Pre-heat oven to 350°F/180°C/Gas Mark 4.
Whisk egg white until very stiff. Add the sugar and nuts. Stir in the
   ground rice and orange rind. Divide into ten pieces. Roll into rounds
   and place on the rice paper, well spaced out, flatten and bake for 20–
   25 minutes in centre of oven. When almost cold, remove from tray
   and trim rice paper. Store in airtight tin.

SCONES (CHEESE)

Makes 8–10

4 oz. gluten free plain flour
1 teaspoon salt
1 teaspoon gluten free baking powder

2 oz. margarine
4 oz. grated cheese
2 eggs   Little milk

Pre-heat oven to 400°F/200°C/Gas Mark 6. Follow method for oven
   scones on p.80, adding cheese after margarine, and eggs and milk
   beaten together. Bake for 20–25 mins. Serve hot.

ICINGS

BUTTER ICING

6 oz. icing sugar
3 oz. butter
A little milk

Sift icing sugar into a bowl. Beat butter until soft and gradually beat into icing sugar, then add a little milk until it is the right consistency.

Variations:

Chocolate: Add 1–1½ oz. melted chocolate *or* 1 level tablespoon cocoa powder dissolved in a little hot water (this should be allowed to cool before it is added to the mixture).

Mocha: Add 1 level teaspoon cocoa powder and 2 level teaspoons instant coffee, dissolved in a little hot water. Allow to cool before adding to the mixture.

Coffee: Add 2 level teaspoons instant coffee in hot water. Allow to cool and add to the mixture.

CARAMEL FUDGE ICING

(For 9–9½ in. cake)

1 oz. butter
2 tablespoons golden syrup
1 tablespoon milk

1 teaspoon vanilla essence
8 oz. icing sugar
1 teaspoon ground cinnamon

Heat butter and golden syrup in a saucepan over moderate heat for 2 minutes. Add milk then remove from heat and stir in vanilla essence. Sift half the icing sugar and cinnamon into saucepan and stir well. Sift the rest and add to mixture.

Pour icing over cake and smooth surface with spatula dipped in hot water to give good finish.

MILK CHOCOLATE ICING

(Sufficient to fill and coat 7 in. sandwich cake)

2½ oz. margarine
4 tablespoons cocoa
8 oz. sifted icing sugar
3 tablespoons hot milk
1 teaspoon vanilla essence

Melt margarine, blend in cocoa then stir in icing sugar, milk and
    essence.
Beat until smooth and thick.

QUICKIE CAKE FROSTING

(A quick and delightful frosting for a sponge)

2 oz. margarine
2 oz. brown sugar
2 oz. chopped nuts

2 tablespoons double cream
1 teaspoon vanilla essence

Melt together the margarine and sugar. Remove from heat and add
    chopped nuts, cream and vanilla. Mix well.
Spread on warm 7 in. sponge cake and put under grill for 2–3 minutes
    until bubbly.

Variation:
Use ½ cup shredded coconut instead of chopped nuts, but use a little
    more cream.

WATER ICING

8 oz. icing sugar
2 tablespoons warm water
1 teaspoon pure lemon juice

Put all ingredients into a pan and beat well. Stir over a gentle heat for 1
    minute.

MISCELLANEOUS

BLACKBERRY AND APPLE JAM (SEEDLESS)

4 lb. blackberries
1½ lb. apples, peeled, cored
and cut up
Water
Sugar

Boil blackberries in a little water until soft. Strain.
Pulp the apples in ½ pint water. Combine apple pulp with blackberry
   juice.
When combined, measure the quantity and add 1 lb. sugar to every pint
   of pulp/liquid.
Dissolve sugar over a low heat then bring to the boil. Continue to boil
   until the setting point is reached (about 15 minutes).
Pour into warm jars and seal.

BLACKCURRANT JAM

6 lb. blackcurrants (no stalks
but leave on tails)
4 pints water
12 lb. preserving, granulated
and demerara sugar (mixed)

Boil blackcurrants in the water in a large pan for 20 minutes. Warm the
   sugar and add to the fruit. Bring to boil and boil hard for 5 minutes or
   until setting point is reached (220°F). Pot into warmed jars and cover.

The quantities can be adjusted for smaller amounts.

This jam makes very good blackcurrant 'tea' and can be used to ease
   colds and coughs. To 2 teaspoons of blackcurrant jam, pour on boiling
   water in a mug.

GREEN TOMATO RELISH

3 lb. green tomatoes
8 onions
2 cucumbers
1 green pepper
1 red pepper
Salt

2 lb. sugar
2 pints malt vinegar
2 tablespoons plain flour
2 tablespoons curry powder
1 tablespoon powdered
mustard

Cut vegetables finely and sprinkle with 1 tablespoon salt and leave to
stand overnight. Strain off most of liquid. Put vegetables in pan with
sugar and vinegar, bring to boil, simmer for 1 hour.
Blend flour, curry powder and mustard with little vinegar liquid, add to
pan and simmer for another 30 minutes. Put in warm jars and seal.

LEMON CHEESE

4 oz. butter
8 oz. sugar

3 eggs
Rind and juice of 2 lemons

Melt butter and sugar in a pan and add lemon juice and finely grated
lemon rind and stir in the beaten eggs. Heat gently, stirring
occasionally, until sugar has dissolved and until it thickens. Pour into
small clean dry jars and cover immediately.

RUNNER BEAN CHUTNEY

2 lb. runner beans (chopped)
1½ lb. onions (finely chopped)
1½ pints malt vinegar
1 teaspoon turmeric

1 teaspoon dry mustard
3 tablespoons cornflour
2 lb. demerara sugar
Salt

Cook the beans in salted water until tender. Strain.
Cook onions in 1 pint of vinegar until tender then add the beans and
cook for 15 minutes. Mix turmeric, mustard, cornflour and a little salt
with the remaining vinegar and add with the sugar to the beans and
onions. Boil gently for a further 15 minutes.
When cool, pot, and when cold, seal the jars. Use jars that have been
scalded and left to cool.

SCOTTISH CREAM (OR IRISH)

1 dessertspoon coffee powder
1 × 14 oz. tin evaporated milk
1 × 14 oz. tin condensed milk

1 teaspoon vanilla essence
2 teaspoons glycerine
1½ cups Scottish (or Irish) whisky

Mix coffee powder with a little hot water until dissolved. Leaving the
whisky until last, put all ingredients in mixing bowl. Mix well (use a
blender if you have one to make sure there are no lumps). Bottle and
seal.

SWEET UNCOOKED PICKLE

1 lb. stoned dates
1 lb. sultanas
1 lb. peeled and cored apples
1 lb. onions
10 oz. brown sugar

1 pint vinegar
1 teaspoon salt
Pinch of pepper
¾ oz. pickling spice

Mince the first four ingredients together and mix with sugar and
vinegar. Add salt and pepper and spice tied in a muslin bag. Stand
for 24 hours.
Remove spice and pot and seal.

UNCOOKED CHUTNEY

1 lb. dates
1 lb. sultanas
1 lb. cooking apples, peeled and cored*
1 lb. onions*
1 lb. dark brown sugar

¾ pint vinegar
1 heaped teaspoon salt
Good pinch cayenne pepper
1 oz. pickling spice (optional)
(*prepared weight)

Mince dates, sultanas, apples and onions and place together in large
bowl. Add remaining ingredients (put spice in muslin if used).
Stir well, cover and leave for 24 hours, stirring occasionally.
Remove spice and bottle.
This chutney can be stored in one large glass jar, taking small amounts
to fill a smaller jar as necessary. Delicious with cold meat, cheese and
poultry. Keeps indefinitely. If a sweeter chutney is preferred, leave
out the spice. Avoids the smell of hot vinegar around the house.